STRATEGIC PLANNING
FOR ACADEMIC LIBRARIES

STRATEGIC PLANNING FOR ACADEMIC LIBRARIES

A Step-by-Step Guide

Gregory C. Thompson

Harish Maringanti

Rick Anderson

Catherine B. Soehner

AND

Alberta Comer

ALA Editions

CHICAGO | 2019

© 2019 by the American Library Association

Extensive effort has gone into ensuring the reliability of the information in this book; however, the publisher makes no warranty, express or implied, with respect to the material contained herein.

ISBN: 978-0-8389-1893-7 (paper)

Library of Congress Cataloging in Publication Control Number: 2019019627

Cover design by Karen Sheets de Gracia. Text design in the Chaparral, Gotham, and Bell Gothic typefaces.

♾ This paper meets the requirements of ANSI/NISO Z39.48-1992 (Permanence of Paper).

Printed in the United States of America

23 22 21 20 19   5 4 3 2 1

Contents

APPENDIXES

Introduction
Why Engage in Strategic Planning?

The goal of this book is to help academic libraries do three things:

1. Plan and prepare for a successful strategic planning process.
2. Implement a successful strategic planning process.
3. Assess the success of both the process and the resulting plan.

Strategic planning, as defined in the *Business Dictionary* (n.d.), is "a systematic process of envisioning a desired future and translating this vision into broadly defined goals or objectives." Envisioning—and creating a roadmap for—this future through a strategic planning process involves several planning stages. Each chapter of this book is focused on one stage of the process, with each chapter divided into three sections. The first section of each chapter discusses the planning stage in general terms, covering overarching principles and common challenges and issues; the second section provides a case study, showing how one institution, the J. Willard Marriott Library at the University of Utah, handled that stage of the process; the third section examines the lessons learned by the staff of the Marriott Library during that stage. The authors hope that by blending a theoretical foundation with concrete examples, this book will provide both an essential conceptual footing and real-life illustrations that will prove helpful to other libraries considering a strategic planning project.

Why Engage in Strategic Planning?

When it comes to strategic planning, the most important initial question is not "how," but rather "whether," and if so, "why." As with many organizational projects—especially large-scale ones that will draw deeply on the organization's fund of staff time and energy—it is crucial to know from the beginning what problem or problems the project is intended to solve.

Corrall outlines reasons for strategic planning, including:

1. To clarify (the organization's) purpose and objectives;
2. To determine directions and priorities;
3. To encourage a broader-based longer-term view;
4. To identify critical issues and constraints;
5. To provide a framework for policy and decisions;
6. To inform resource allocation and utilization. (Corrall 2000, 2)

Nearly twenty years after the publication of Corrall's book, these reasons for strategic planning remain valid. However, there is also another powerful motivator prompting library organizations to engage in strategic planning. In an environment in which the library's traditional value propositions are being undermined by cultural and technological change and challenged by proliferating competitors for patrons' time and attention, academic libraries must respond successfully to the overarching question of how to remain central to their home institutions' missions and priorities while continuing to innovate and deliver desired research information and services to their users. To remain relevant to their users and mission-critical to their sponsoring institutions, academic libraries must both position themselves strategically in alignment with the goals and priorities of those institutions and respond to the real and demonstrable needs of their users—while also setting a bold but achievable vision for the future.

As libraries position themselves to align with institutional goals, they may discover that these goals are a moving target because universities are facing significant challenges to their ability to accomplish core missions. Growing (or, in some cases, diminishing) student populations; tightening resources and revenue flows (especially for state-supported universities); and changing expectations on the part of the public, state legislatures, and academia's direct client group—students—all contribute to these challenges. From all sides, universities are under pressure to "do more with less." With university budgets shrinking and competition increasing across campus for allocations from that shrinking budget—and in light of the popular perception that necessary information can largely be found online via Google and other platforms—libraries may find themselves needing increasingly to advocate for their very existence. As libraries adjust to changing user needs and perceptions as well as to shifting university priorities, they must find new ways to remain relevant and mission-critical.

Libraries contemplating this changing educational landscape might reasonably conclude that change is needed within their own organizations if they are to remain essential to their host institutions. Some additional important reasons, then, for developing a strategic plan might include:

- Identifying and illuminating the challenges facing the library and its host institution.
- Increasing institutional awareness of the library's value propositions.
- Increasing the library's institutional understanding of users' perceptions and use patterns.
- Improving understanding within the library of the larger institutional environment.
- Revealing possible strategies for addressing the issues the library is facing.

Strategic planning is, in short, designed to help the library *implement informed change.*

This raises a secondary question: is strategic planning a one-time effort, or a permanent program consisting of iterative tasks and projects, designed not only to put the library on a solid course for the future, but to keep it there as well?

The answer, of course, is that it can be either. The authors' recommendation, however, is that strategic planning be adopted as a permanent feature of the library's organizational culture. This does not mean that the library must always be in the middle of creating a new strategic plan—however, as we shall see, it is possible to create both a cyclical program of periodic strategic plans (i.e., one leads into the next) and to maintain an ongoing posture of assessment and review that keeps strategic plans appropriately flexible and responsive to changing realities.

The decision to undertake a strategic planning process, and to incorporate strategic planning into the permanent culture of the library organization, will always represent a significant commitment of time and energy. It is to be expected that embarking on this effort will challenge the organization—it is in the nature of strategic plans that they are disruptive, self-critical exercises that are intended to bring significant informed change to an organization and perhaps even to its core structure. For library faculty and staff, the tasks involved in the strategic planning process itself will be experienced as add-ons to current responsibilities and, therefore, it must be presented to them with skill and sensitivity, by means of processes that invite their input and feedback and that are informed by their perspectives. Inevitably, a serious engagement in strategic planning will commit the library to a long and laborious process—one that can pay large dividends for the library and its users if undertaken skillfully, thoughtfully, and with sensitivity to the impacts of the process on all involved.

THE MARRIOTT LIBRARY'S STORY

Answering the "Why"

In 2014, the J. Willard Marriott Library embarked on a strategic planning project with an initiative titled "Imagine U: Creating YOUR Library of the Future." The goal was to envision a "desired future" and to create a roadmap to get there, taking into account a complex array of environmental, political, and fiscal realities. The Library's prior strategic plan had covered the period 2011–2013 (appendix A). With the arrival of a new dean in August 2013 and with a new university president in place, it seemed an ideal time to draft new strategic directions. In addition, the university's new administration was leading the campus in redefining the University of Utah's role as the flagship research institution for the state of Utah. Given the university's history of innovation (e.g., as a national leader for technology commercialization, entrepreneurship, and video game design), its international reputation for genetics research, and its pioneering work with artificial hearts, it was deemed time to refocus and re-envision the institution's future.

Initial Lessons Learned

As the strategic planning process got under way, the Marriott Library administration and staff learned a number of important lessons. One of these was that, although no one expected the strategic planning process to be easy or quick, it turned out to be even more labor-intensive than had been anticipated. In significant part, this was because all levels of library staff were involved from the earliest stages of the process. No adjustments were made in the staff's existing duties to accommodate this new work, and the strategic planning tasks were thus added on top of schedules and duties that were, in many cases, already heavy. In hindsight, those staff who were assigned particularly active and demanding roles in the process should have had their workloads adjusted by either temporarily sharing work with others or putting some projects on hold.

A second lesson learned was that undertaking strategic planning with a new dean made the process very different from what it would have been if the dean had been in the position for a longer period. Because the dean was new, she was still learning about the Library and its staff, projects, and priorities during the same time that those things were under strategic evaluation. Because she was new to the University, she had to learn to navigate campus structures and rules and to master campus norms and processes (e.g., how to obtain Institutional Review Board [IRB] approval for surveys and the required procedures to hire an outside consulting firm). Assigning someone with more experience at the Marriott Library to guide her through university red tape might have expedited the process and made it easier to keep it on schedule. On the positive side, the new dean viewed Library services through fresh eyes; she was unconstrained by longstanding investment in existing processes and was thus more responsive to ideas that might have seemed far-fetched to a dean with more time in the position.

All in all, the Library has found, and continues to find, strategic planning to be a useful mapping, planning, and evaluation tool for future development. Strategic planning has played an important role in meeting current challenges and in developing creative and flexible new pathways into the future.

1

Preplanning

ONCE A LIBRARY HAS DECIDED TO ENGAGE IN STRATEGIC PLANning, the first stage of the process is preplanning. Preplanning for strategic planning may sound redundant and, technically speaking, it might be. However, this is the stage at which the foundation is laid for how the process will be conducted, and therefore an essential element of every successful strategic plan. Because the end product of an effective strategic planning process is certain to be at least somewhat disruptive and to have a concrete impact on all library stakeholders, decisions made at the earliest stages can be of great importance—some of these will determine the trajectory of the entire process or elements of it. In other words, when it comes to strategic planning, "planning to plan" is crucial.

Preplanning involves several considerations:

Timing: When will the process begin, and what will be the target dates throughout the process?

Leadership and management: Who will start the process, and who will guide the process to its conclusion?

Context: What can be learned and perhaps carried forward from the current strategic plan?

Audience: Who are the library's stakeholders, and how will they be brought on board?

Institutional alignment: How will the library's plan track with the strategic priorities of the host institution?

An overview of these factors may prove beneficial.

Timing. Here there are two questions: first, when is the right time for the strategic planning process to begin? Second, how long should the process take, and what will be the inflection points in the planning timeline? The answers to these questions will vary from situation to situation and will be informed by such considerations as the expiration of the current strategic plan; the announcement and implementation of new university priorities or strategic initiatives; the arrival of a new library dean or director; or significant developments within the library profession (or in higher education) that need to be addressed. Although it is essential to lay out a timeline at the beginning of the process so that progress can be tracked and tasks rationally distributed, it is equally important to provide for a reasonable degree of flexibility in the timeline; unforeseen events and complications are inevitable, and a good planning timeline will be able to bend as needed (within reason) without breaking.

Leadership and management. It is important to bear in mind that "leadership" and "management" are not the same thing. Introducing the project and setting it in motion is the task of a leader, ideally the library dean or director. It needs to be clear to all stakeholders—especially the library staff—that the strategic planning process is proceeding either under the direct oversight of the library's dean or director or at least with his or her full support. However, in most libraries it would be folly for the dean or director to manage the entire process. Although he or she will maintain close and active oversight and will have hands-on involvement to varying degrees throughout the planning period, he or she will need to delegate most of the day-to-day management of the process to other administrators and managers. In some cases, it may make sense to form a new committee or working group dedicated to strategic planning. In other cases, libraries may have existing organizational structures that can be charged with moving the plan forward. Either way, it is important to have engaged participation from staff who are willing to commit for the long term, because strategic planning is not just a one-time event, but an ongoing and sometimes iterative process.

Context. As the new plan is being conceptualized, it is important to review the previous one (if one exists), asking what the library can learn from it and from the process that created that plan. Will the new plan represent a continuation of the general directions laid out in that one, a new set of goals coupled with a redirection of efforts, or, more likely, some combination of both? How did the library change in response to the previous plan? What were the intended outcomes, and—importantly—what were the unintended ones? Is the library now more aligned with campus priorities than it was before the previous plan was implemented, or less so? Although the new strategic plan should not be written while constantly looking over one's shoulder at the old one, looking back at previous efforts, especially at the beginning of the planning process, can prevent repeating mistakes and duplicating failed initiatives. If the library does not have a strategic plan in place, it is still important to consider what changes the library has undergone in the previous few years and what lessons were learned.

Audience. For whom will the new plan be written? Inevitably, it will be aimed at multiple audiences: its primary readers will be library employees, the people who will be most directly affected by it—but it should also communicate the library's vision and goals clearly to campus administration and to interested library patrons; therefore, it will need to be written in a clear and direct manner that avoids library jargon wherever possible. Additionally, and perhaps even more importantly, is the question of how to get stakeholder buy-in both for the planning process itself and for the changes that will result from that process. Here the primary stakeholders are library employees, but it is also essential to solicit the input of the library's users, including faculty, staff, students, administrators, and donors. For some academic libraries, particularly those embedded in public institutions of higher education, it may also be wise to include input from the surrounding community.

Institutional Alignment. The last question to consider is how and to what degree the library should tie its strategic goals to those of the university. Do the university's goals have a natural overlap with the library's mission (e.g., student success)? What if some goals of the university are not a natural fit? Additionally, what if the library has goals that the university does not expressly state? Can and should these goals be tied more explicitly to the university's strategic plans and priorities? If the library has goals that seem to be in tension with those of the university, to what degree should they be adjusted to bring them into greater harmony?

All these questions are important to consider from the beginning of the strategic planning process. How they are answered will vary from library to library, depending in significant part on such factors as the political environment on campus, the strength of the library's existing relationship with campus administration, the degree to which the library enjoys broad support from faculty and students, and so forth.

THE MARRIOTT LIBRARY'S STORY

Preplanning

Looking at these factors through the lens of the Marriott Library's experience may also prove beneficial.

Timing. For the Marriott Library, the decision to engage in strategic planning was prompted not only by the arrival of a new dean, but also by the fact that the Library's previous plan had expired the year prior to her arrival. The 2011–2013 plan had been developed under the previous dean and leadership team, and a more dynamic strategic plan was desired by the current administration. In addition, as stated earlier, the University of Utah's new administration, including the new university president and senior vice president of academic affairs, was rethinking campus priorities. Library administration decided that "business as usual" in the Library was not a sustainable approach and felt that the emerging campus priorities presented an opportunity to rethink the Library's strategic plan.

Leadership and management. At the Marriott Library, the strategic planning process began with the Library's Executive Council (EC), which consisted of the dean, associate deans, and directors, as well as elected representatives from the faculty and staff. To begin the pre-planning process, the dean organized a retreat for the EC, the purpose of which was to construct a conceptual framework for the new strategic plan. The retreat marked the first time that the EC had met for such an event and the meeting was held off campus, an unusual occurrence. All attendees were given assignments ahead of time designed to jump-start the thinking process. The dean also provided the EC with an agenda (appendix B) outlining the goals, questions, and schedule for the retreat. The uniqueness of this arrangement, along with the preparation expected of each member, signaled to all participants that the Library was taking the strategic planning process very seriously.

In preparation for the retreat, attendees were asked to read three articles on strategic planning. The first reading, "The Strategic Plan is Dead, Long Live Strategy," by O'Donovan and Flower (2013), advocated abandoning predictions about what the future might bring and, instead, treating the entire organization as a team that was experimenting its way to success. The authors argued for the necessity of creating a plan that would be dynamic and would "be adaptive and directive, that emphasizes learning and control, and that reclaims the value of strategic thinking for the world that now surrounds us" (para. 7). The authors emphasized that "creating strategies that are truly adaptive requires that we give up on many long-held assumptions" and "abandon our focus on predictions and shift into rapid prototyping and experimentation so that we learn quickly about what actually works" (para. 9).

The second reading, Birdsall's "Strategic Planning in Academic Libraries: A Political Perspective" (1997), addressed the importance of soliciting a diversity of viewpoints and encouraging full and broad participation in the planning process, as well as forming a coalition among key library stakeholders. It also advocated creating persuasive planning documents to use as marketing tools to advance library objectives. The author proposed three political strategies that would optimize planning outcomes: (1) build upon the diversity of stakeholders, (2) form alliances and coalitions to advance library interests, and (3) market a persuasive planning document.

The third reading, Germano and Stretch-Stephenson's "Strategic Value Planning for Libraries," warned of nine factors that could undermine the strength of a strategic plan:

1. Poor employee engagement
2. Poor communication
3. Lack of clarity in terms of goals and expected outcomes
4. Inadequate leadership development within organizations
5. Insufficient speed and adaptability when refinements are required
6. Slow decision-making
7. Resource inadequacy
8. Lack of attention to customer needs
9. Non-alignment across functional areas (Germano and Stretch-Stephenson 2012, 74)

The authors stressed that "without the willingness to adapt plans during execution, virtually any strategic plan is destined to perform inadequately or fail. Because most strategic plans take place over sustained periods of time, planning without adaptation is the strategic equivalent of painting oneself into a corner" (Germano and Stretch-Stephenson 2012, 75).

In addition to the three articles, the retreat's participants reviewed seven strategic plans that had been created at a variety of other libraries (Cornell University, University of Kansas, Purdue University, UCLA, New York University, Carnegie Library of Pittsburgh, and Seattle Public Library), each providing a different example of style, format, and focus. Drawing on the insights contained in the articles and strategic plans, EC members began the process of creating a road map to guide the Library's endeavors in the coming years.

One early question that the EC discussed at the retreat was, "Why have a strategic plan?" Although corporations have engaged in strategic planning since the 1940s, libraries began much later, with the Association of College and Research Libraries (ACRL) instituting strategic planning for its own mission and vision in 1981 (Brown and Gonzalez 2007). Many libraries subsequently followed suit. The EC discussed the positive outcomes of strategic planning, including being better prepared for changes that were occurring in academic libraries. The EC also considered the limitations of strategic planning, including the inability to predict the future, the difficulty of writing a plan that covered multiple years when library users' needs would be rapidly changing, and the challenge of concisely defining organizational values. Even with these recognized limitations, the EC concluded that it was important to engage in strategic planning to envision a "desired future" and create a road map leading to it. With the conclusion of the retreat, the strategic planning process was officially underway.

Context. To ensure that the organization learned what it could from its previous planning process, the EC began by assessing the execution and success of the Marriott Library's 2011–2013 strategic plan (appendix A). Those in the group who had worked at the Library during the creation of that strategic plan agreed it worked well in some areas, particularly by identifying priorities and laying out concrete steps and guidelines. Also, organizational enhancement had been included, with human capital a priority. However, there were drawbacks as well, chiefly with regard to stakeholder buy-in, which had largely been neglected during the previous planning process.

Audience. The previous plan had been developed by a small group of top administrators with little input from others inside or (especially) outside the library. Although feedback sessions had been held, most strategies had already been put in place, and little buy-in had been generated with middle management, front-line employees, or users. The EC felt that an important opportunity had been missed because the Library's users had not been asked what they needed, and indeed had not been included in the planning process at all. The EC felt strongly that staff and users should play an active role in the new strategic planning process.

Institutional Alignment. The EC felt that another problem with the 2011–2013 plan was that it was not mapped to the university's goals. It had proven difficult to ascertain how the Library supported the university, making it problematic to provide statistics in support of requests for new funding from the university administration.

Here the Marriott Library was fortunate in its timing. Mapping the Library's strategic plan to the university's goals might have proven difficult had the project been undertaken earlier because the university was undertaking its own institution-wide strategic planning at about the same time as the Library. A new Senior Vice President for Academic Affairs—a position analogous to that of Provost at other institutions—had arrived at roughly the same time as the Library dean in 2013, and a new university president had been inaugurated only a few months prior to that. Fortuitously, the university announced its strategic goals shortly before the Library began formulating its own strategic plan. Additionally, the university's four goals were both broad and concise, making it relatively easy for the Library to see how its mission and goals could be aligned with them. The university's goals (appendix C) were:

1. Promote student success to transform lives.
2. Develop and transfer new knowledge.
3. Engage communities to improve health and quality of life.
4. Ensure long-term viability of the university.

The Library embraced these four goals as a guide, changing only slightly the language in number three, and adding two or three points under each goal. In the case of the third goal, the Marriott Library found that the campus-wide version fit poorly with its own scope of mission, and therefore omitted the phrase "engage communities," retaining "to improve health and quality of life."

This allowed the Library's goal to fit with the university's goal of promoting community health, while keeping the Library's local focus on maintaining a healthy learning and work environment and fostering diversity and inclusion.

As the Library progressed through its strategic planning process, final reports and the data gathered suggested that something was still missing from the Library's draft plan. For example, many of the surveys and focus groups made clear that some respondents were simply unaware of services and resources already provided by the Library. Additionally, Library employees had indicated that salaries were a problem that needed to be addressed and that they were interested in more development, mentoring, and training opportunities. As a result, two more goals were added to the Library strategic plan:

- Increase awareness of Library services and resources.
- Enhance Library employee potential.

The Library's final strategic goals are in appendix D.

Lessons Learned

The preplanning process was instructive for the Library in several different ways. On the positive side, the EC retreat brought clarity to the planning process and helped the EC and the new dean solidify their relationship, as everyone worked together for a common purpose. The EC was the appropriate group to start the planning process because it was open to the idea of creating change, an important aspect of strategic planning, and it could visualize the Library at a high level—not just from the perspective of its own administrative units.

Conversely, there were things that the Library should have done differently in the preplanning process. For example, one voice missing from the EC retreat was that of the students. Although students were involved in subsequent phases of the planning process, in hindsight, the strategic plan would have benefited from having them involved from the very beginning. When students joined the effort later they offered wise counsel and insight and added much to the conversation and decision-making process.

It also became clear in hindsight that the EC, in its preplanning work, had underestimated the time it would take to complete the entire process. Eighteen months passed between the beginning of the EC's retreat and completion of the strategic planning document, a much longer period than what was initially anticipated. Writing survey instruments, gathering feedback from across campus (including multiple in-person focus groups), and then writing and rewriting reports and other documents proved to be time-consuming. All those measures to gather feedback were worth the time and effort, but the process of informing staff and users would have gone more smoothly and been accomplished with less frustration if the activities had been based on a more realistic timeline. Instead, the planning leaders were required to push deadlines back on multiple occasions.

One of the most positive outcomes of the preplanning process turned out to be the mapping of the Library's goals to those of the university. This has proved beneficial in ways the EC could not have imagined at the time of its retreat. Franklin (2012, 105) observed that "a strategic plan and organizational structure based on institutional mission changes the focus of library staff from the library and its functions to its users and their needs." Franklin added that it also "generates campus buy-in" (106). Saunders (2015) noted that aligning a library's plan with the university's goals improves decision-making about prioritizing and allocating resources, and the Marriott Library has found that true.

Since the university's strategic goals were unveiled, campus administration has required that budget reports, requests for ongoing financial support, and requests for new initiatives all be presented in the context of the university's strategic goals. Having the Library's strategic plan mapped to university goals and structuring the Library's internal reporting to correlate with the strategic plan has provided powerful and convincing support for requests to the university. It has also made it easier to write reports and proposals, because the necessary justifications are easily formulated. Dillon's 2008 piece, which foreshadowed the Marriott Library's situation by five years—suggested that "the future of academic libraries . . . [will] be determined by the extent to which they amplify the mission of their host institutions and, ultimately, the mission of the university system at a national and international level." (2008, 54).

In retrospect, the preplanning process was essential to developing the Library's strategic goals. Bringing the Library's leadership team together at the beginning of the process set the tone for everything that followed: strategic planning would be a Library-wide effort and one that welcomed feedback from all stakeholders.

2

Facilitation

THE NEXT IMPORTANT ISSUE TO CONSIDER IS WHO WILL CARRY out the strategic planning process itself. Three possible strategies to consider are: (1) appointing facilitators from within the library; (2) engaging facilitators from inside the university but outside the library; and (3) hiring consultants from outside the university. Before making this important decision, the following questions should be considered:

- How much funding is available for the strategic planning process?
- What deliverables does the library expect to see at the end of the process?
- Do library employees have the expertise needed to lead focus groups and to create and execute surveys—and to analyze the resulting data? If so, do these employees have sufficiently flexible schedules to allow them to plan and lead this time-consuming project? And, importantly, will library patrons and employees feel free to give their honest opinions about the library if the person leading the discussion is a library employee?
- Are there available personnel on campus with the objectivity, perspective, ability, time, and interest necessary to effectively carry out the project?

Answers to these questions will help determine feedback mechanisms, the amount of time and expertise that may be needed to gather and interpret data, and, ultimately, which of the three facilitation options will be the best choice for your library.

Nutefall (2015, 6) suggested that "once the decision is made to use a facilitator one of the first questions should be whether to look internal to the organization (faculty member, HR) or external (outside consultants)." There are a number of reasons to hire outside consultants; one of the most important is that doing so frees staff to more fully and freely participate in the planning process. But there are also compelling reasons to draw upon campus or in-house resources, such as cost avoidance—although here it is important to point out the reality of opportunity cost, which can be significant when staff are redirected from their usual duties to oversee or carry out planning efforts. The right answer to the question of who should facilitate the strategic planning process will vary from library to library, depending on financial constraints and available resources, as well as many other factors.

These three general strategies of facilitation: by library employees, by university employees, or by external consultants—are examined below.

Library Facilitators

The chief benefit of having existing library employees serve as in-house facilitators is the avoidance of direct (i.e., financial) cost. Another (mixed) benefit is that in-house facilitators know the organization and its employees well; this is helpful in that it minimizes the amount of time needed to get to know the organization's culture and existing workflows but can be detrimental in that the facilitators may have well-established opinions as to what should and should not change, which may cloud their perceptions. As mentioned above, another significant downside to using internal staff as facilitators is the time and energy it will divert from regular library tasks.

If library employees are tasked with conducting the strategic planning process, there are additional questions to resolve prior to undertaking that initiative. It is highly likely that the library will form a strategic planning committee whose members would serve as facilitators. Without such a committee, it would be difficult to establish a cohesive team to take on the strategic planning process. Questions that should be addressed while forming the planning committee would include:

- Who should chair the committee? (In particular, should the chair be a library administrator or a member of the line staff or faculty? There will be pros and cons to either approach.)
- How many members will be on the committee?

- Will the committee be responsible for all aspects of the project, including writing and administering surveys and/or leading focus groups? (And if not, who will assume those duties, and how and by whom will they be managed?)
- Will the committee draft the final report? (And again, if not, who will?)
- Will committee members be given reduced responsibilities in their primary areas of work for the duration of the strategic planning process? If so, who will take on their work? If not, how will committee members fit these extra duties into their everyday workflows?

The answers to these questions will depend on a number of factors that will vary from library to library, including the size of the library's staff and the anticipated length of time to complete the project. It will be important to answer them as early in the process as possible.

Matthews (2005) discussed strategic planning that was facilitated by a planning committee made up of library staff from three levels: administrative decision-makers, middle management, and front-line staff. He argued for including staff from all three areas because they each play a unique but important role in the library: administrators have an overarching perspective on library operations and directions; middle managers are experienced in translating policy into tasks and workflows; and front-line staff provide unique insights about their specific areas of expertise and have the most direct responsibility for turning policy into action. Because front-line staff are also usually those who interact most often and directly with patrons, they have an invaluable perspective on the real-world effects of library policies and practices. Matthews also suggested that "members of the planning committee should be selected for their skills and abilities to make a contribution to the overall plan" (89), and that a single individual should be responsible for writing the plan; however, once a draft is written he emphasized that it should be shared with key stakeholders before final editing. All in all, Matthews recommended having a committee of eight to ten members, made up of upper, middle, and front-line employees who could provide a diversity of perspectives and skill sets that would contribute to the strategic planning process.

Some library directors may, for various reasons (e.g., cost, time constraints, competing commitments, administrative style, etc.), choose to write the strategic plan on their own, without extensive outside feedback. But because buy-in from library employees and users is so essential to the effective execution and successful outcomes of a new strategic plan, in most instances employees and users should be active participants throughout the strategic planning process as well as in its implementation and assessment. The authors strongly recommend that the strategic planning process include the participation of all members of the library organization—at least as respondents and informers, if not always as facilitators.

Campus Facilitators

If campus personnel from outside the library will carry out the strategic planning, questions that should be addressed at the outset would include:

- Who on campus has the expertise and time to take on these roles?
- What roles, if any, will library staff have in the process?
- Who will manage the work of the external facilitators (the library dean or director, the strategic planning task force, or some other leadership group)?

Often campus human resources personnel have the expertise to lead a strategic planning project, although faculty or staff from one of the university's colleges might have that expertise as well. It is important to verify up front that whoever is chosen not only has the expertise but also the time and interest to take on the project. Expectations should be discussed ahead of time with both external facilitators and campus personnel and mutually agreed upon using a memorandum of understanding.

Jennifer Nutefall, University Librarian at Santa Clara University, made the case for hiring someone from campus to help with the planning process, while pointing out that although a campus consultant might lead the strategic planning process, most likely he or she will not have time to manage all aspects of the project. Nutefall (2015) suggested that activities be split between library employees and the campus consultant. For example, although the campus consultant might lead focus groups and collect and analyze survey data, library employees could take charge of writing survey questions and handling at least some aspects of marketing.

Having used a facilitator from her campus' human resources department, Nutefall (2015, 2) found that one benefit of this approach was the facilitator's "familiarity with the university combined with a limited knowledge of the library." She found that the facilitator's non-library perspective ensured that the terminology used in the final document would be more easily understood by audiences outside the library. Furthermore, Nutefall said that the facilitator helped the committee "pare down complicated topics into easily understood goals or objectives" (5). She also found that having a non-library facilitator allowed library employees to be full participants in the planning process because they were not also serving in that role.

Germano and Stretch-Stephenson (2012, 82) suggested that an additional reason for having campus facilitators from outside the library lead the strategic planning process was that libraries needed to "imagine themselves in the eyes of the patron and not merely in ways they assume patrons think or feel about their library." Although someone who is not part of the library staff can make this point gently but authoritatively, it might be more difficult for a library colleague to do the same.

External Consultants

If the library decides to hire consultants from outside of campus, it is especially important that expectations be discussed ahead of time and mutually agreed upon using a formal contract or memorandum of agreement. It is important to remember that however involved the consultant will be in the strategic planning process, the final "product" will be the responsibility of the library and university and should be geared toward the needs of local constituents. This final product may or may not end up reflecting the consultant's concept of the "ideal" library or views on best practices. Hinton (2012, 16) argued that consultants "cannot 'tell' an institution what it should achieve with a strategic plan" because "without the ownership developed through a participatory process, the likelihood of a failed plan is enormous, as are incidences of process sabotage and simple non-implementation." She added that "a qualified consultant is a master of the process, but institutional staff are masters of the content" (17). External consultants should always step away from the process before the final deliverable has been created; it is the library leadership who will ultimately take responsibility for the content of the strategic plan.

When choosing potential external consultants, the following questions should be considered and should be included in the contract or memo of understanding:

- What deliverables can the library expect to see at the end of the process?
- How many days will be needed for each specific phase of the project?
- What is the daily consultation fee? This will be important information to request, along with a total quote for the project as a whole, in case the project takes longer than anticipated and additional consultant time is needed.
- What is included in the consultant's fee? Is travel included in the overall cost? If not, it may be easier to track and plan for these costs by having a specific price for each aspect of travel. For example, "$600 for airplane travel" is much easier to plan for than a "round trip airplane ticket." Even if the contract says that

"round trip airplane ticket, coach fare," prices can vary widely among airlines and even from day to day within a single airline.

- What happens if the project is not completed on time, or if deliverables are not produced by the agreed-upon deadline? Will there be penalties?
- If the library wishes to contract for more work, such as holding additional focus groups, what would the consultant charge? Would it be at the same daily rate?
- How and when will the consultant invoice the library? Often the cost is divided up in phases, with a percentage due after each phase. It is unwise to pay all fees up front because it may be difficult to recoup the money if things do not proceed as anticipated, in which event it would be better to lose some of the investment instead of all of it.
- Are incidental costs such as duplication of printed materials included in the consultants' price quote?
- What will be the role of library staff? Staff members will probably be the ones to advertise the survey and focus group meetings because they are more likely to know how and where to effectively advertise. Staff members also are candidates to provide technical expertise to host the survey because it may be difficult for consultants to gain campus authorization to do so.

As the library begins the process of hiring a consultant, it will be essential to keep in mind what is needed from the consultant, what areas of expertise will be required, and how much time will library employees will be expected to devote to the process. Hinton (2012, 17) suggested that "it is necessary for each institution to evaluate the strengths and weaknesses of any potential consultant and, from that, determine if the 'fit' is the right one" Cohen and Cohen (2003, para 5). stated that "it is easy to hire a consultant, but not as easy to get the proper fit unless you know exactly what that fit must be."

Hinton (2012) outlined several reasons why hiring an outside consultant would be beneficial, including the observation that an experienced consultant balanced "competing voices to ensure the plan reflects the needs and aspirations of all stakeholders, not just those who can dominate a meeting" (17). Mandeville-Gamble's (2016) chapter summarized one argument for using consultants: "one of the main benefits in bringing in consultants, whether from off campus or from university human resources, is that these individuals can act as neutral players who can frame and lead conversations and sidestep a number of the internal political processes" (7). In addition, Cohen and Cohen (2003, para. 4), stated that consultants can "ask the embarrassing questions and take the heat."

Potential consultants may be identified by talking to others in the library world, perhaps from another library that has just completed the process, or through local, regional, or national library associations that often maintain a listing of consultants (Cohen and Cohen 2003).

Facilitators

As mentioned in the first paragraph of this chapter, one of the first major decisions for a library undertaking a strategic planning process is who should lead the project. In the Marriott Library's case, the administration's decision not to use campus facilitators narrowed the options to either hiring an outside consultant to help with the strategic planning process, or conducting the process in-house using library employees.

Given the amount of time and human capital involved with seeking staff and user feedback and then working with the resulting data, and in light of a concern that Library employees might be reluctant to participate if feedback were collected by colleagues, Library administration decided to hire a consultant from outside the university.

Although the Library was not required to issue a competitive request for proposals (RFP), some universities may require one. In any case, touching base with the university's central purchasing office prior to engaging any consultants is important. Even if an RFP is not required, many universities may require approval by other campus entities such as the director of procurement and/or the Office of General Counsel.

After discussion between the Library dean and associate deans, two individuals were chosen who were well-known to several EC members from previous work they had done with the consultants on other projects. The Library dean contacted the consultants to confirm they had relevant experience, could provide positive references, were available during a timeframe that met the Library's needs, and proposed fees that were reasonable and fit both the Library budget and the university's guidelines on consultant fees. Once these prerequisites were met, meetings were scheduled with the consultants.

In August 2014, after the dean's preliminary phone calls with the consultants, the dean and associate deans met with the consultants via telephone conferences. The purpose of these meetings was to define roles and responsibilities for the consultants and the Library, confirm focus group and survey logistics, verify project timelines, identify project documentation, and further define project outcomes. Consultants' roles would include facilitating meetings, drafting discussion guides, creating meeting agendas and surveys, and developing reports. The Library's responsibilities would include approving agendas, designing and distributing surveys, and sending invitations to participate in the surveys. These responsibilities were divided among a wide range of Library employees.

Lessons Learned

Although the Library was pleased with the work of the consultants, more investigation might have deepened the pool of available facilitators. Additionally, it may have proven useful to have asked to see examples of previous work results and consider whether consultant writing styles fit the reports that were to be generated. Even if the same consultants had eventually been hired, ideas generated from discussions with other potential consultants might have proved fruitful and provided the Library with as-yet unknown options.

3

Feedback

THE PREVIOUS CHAPTER DISCUSSED THE IMPORTANCE OF GET-
ting feedback from stakeholders, but what or who are the library's stakeholders? McRae (2017, 3) asserted that "each library organization has specific
groups that exert influence upon it. These groups are the library's 'stakeholders' and it is the library's mission to satisfy the needs of these groups." One
category of stakeholder, then, consists of those people or groups who have
a vested interest in the library's goals and some degree of influence over the
library as an organization. Another category would be those whom the library
directly serves—some of whom will be in positions to exert influence over the
library and some of whom may not.

The stakeholder list is long and includes the library's employees, campus
administrators, faculty, staff, and students. The list may also include donors,
board members, and—especially for libraries serving public institutions of
higher education—members of the larger off-campus community. Each of
these stakeholder groups intersects with library services and resources in a
somewhat different way, and thus each will bring a unique set of perspectives
on the library. Feedback from these diverse groups will provide a broad view
of stakeholder expectations and can help better inform its strategic direction.

Engaging with stakeholders allows the library to discover what users like about the library, what they wish could be changed, and which of their needs are not being met. With this information, the library can then better meet the needs of its constituents. For these reasons and others, gathering stakeholder feedback is of paramount importance in writing a successful strategic plan. Identifying library stakeholders is the first step toward gathering that data.

Once stakeholder groups are identified, the next step is to decide what means will be used to solicit feedback. Two obvious mechanisms for soliciting feedback are surveys and focus groups; both approaches will be discussed in this chapter. However, at the outset it is important to acknowledge that in a university setting, surveys and focus groups may be considered forms of human-subject research. Oversight of such research usually falls under the institution's Institutional Review Board (IRB). An IRB is charged with protecting the rights of people involved in studies conducted by the university; therefore, before soliciting users for feedback, it will be important to first contact the university offices that vet and approve human subject research.

If the library hires outside consultants for strategic planning, the consultants will likely have expertise in writing survey questions, but they will need help with determining the exact information to be solicited. King (2005, 104) noted that "frequently-cited purposes for conducting a survey include evaluating existing services [and] gauging the need for new services." King also pointed out the need to write an engaging introduction to the survey, something to inspire potential subjects to engage with and complete it, and he recommended offering concrete incentives to those who finish the survey. He further cautioned that surveys should be short, clear, and concise and warned against trying to ask too many questions—and, importantly, he urged his readers not to "ask for information without contemplating its usefulness beforehand" (107).

If the strategic planning process is being managed in-house, seek out library staff who have experience in writing survey questions and use their expertise to help draft the survey. King (2005) suggested that those who are creating a survey should ask themselves two questions as they do so:

1. What difference will it make to have the information solicited by the survey?
2. What data would be most beneficial to have in future decision-making?

King (2005) also recommended requesting and reviewing sample survey questions from library interest groups. These might be the library's student advisory board, faculty advisory group, development council, or other similar advisory organizations.

Although surveys are a good way to solicit information from users, focus groups can also provide important qualitative data. Higa-Moore et al. (2002, 86) suggested that "few methods provide the wealth of information gained from actually conversing with patrons." Focus groups can also be used effectively to solicit information from those working in the library.

Although focus groups can be led by library employees, the authors strongly suggest hiring someone from outside the library structure to lead these discussions, even if the overall strategic planning process is being managed by an in-house group. If library employees lead the discussion, attendees may be less likely to reveal their honest opinions. Whether focus group attendees are themselves library employees or users from across campus, they may find it difficult to be critical of the library if the person leading the discussion is a library employee. It may also be difficult for the library employee conducting the survey to remain neutral if the conversation should turn negative.

Although information that is received via surveys or from focus groups can be very helpful to an organization, all responses should remain anonymous. (This also argues against having library employees conduct focus group discussions.) Giving respondents anonymity increases the likelihood of receiving honest responses to the questions; however, anonymity may also increase the likelihood of comments that are critical of colleagues. One person (the dean or an associate dean) should be responsible for reviewing all comments prior to their distribution and removing or redacting those, whether positive or negative, that either name a colleague directly or from which a reader could infer someone's identity. This is true not only for comments from library employees, but for all survey and focus group responses. Keep potentially revealing details of these anonymous responses confidential and share only a report that describes patterns and themes evident in the overall comments.

Once the surveys and focus groups have been completed and the resulting data gathered and synthesized into reports, it is time to create a strategy for distributing the results. One good approach is to start by meeting with each major stakeholder group—faculty, staff, and students—to review the reports prior to any public release. This process is important even if there is low turnout from campus stakeholders. Although most may not take advantage of the opportunity, campus stakeholders should be given the chance to review and discuss the reports. A separate meeting of library employees might be planned that focuses on answers provided by library staff, though it is also important to give the library staff access to the other reports that contain information gathered from campus faculty, staff, and students.

The library dean should also consider holding a separate meeting with central campus administration to review the reports and recommendations prior to public release. This is an important step, as the data can provide a launching point for new initiatives and might provide important support for future funding requests. Informing campus administration of the library leadership's initial read on the data and its implications can help the administration think about the library in different ways and can prepare administrators for new programs and services that may be inspired by the research.

THE MARRIOTT LIBRARY'S STORY

Gathering Feedback

As part of the strategic preplanning process, the Library dean and the two consultants met by phone to identify groups that would be asked to provide feedback as part of the strategic planning process; the dean, in consultation with the associate deans, had previously decided that the process should include all Library employees as well as representatives from the wider campus community, and that information would be gathered through both surveys and focus group meetings.

Approval was obtained from the university's IRB (appendix E) specifically to conduct surveys and focus groups to inform the Library's strategic planning effort. For the strategic planning project, the Marriott Library received an IRB exemption that stated:

> The IRB has administratively reviewed your application and has determined on 9/18/2014 that your project does NOT meet the definitions of Human Subjects Research according to Federal regulations. Therefore, IRB oversight is not required or necessary for your project.
>
> DETERMINATION JUSTIFICATION:
>
> The activity is not a systematic investigation designed to develop or contribute to generalizable knowledge. (University of Utah Institutional Review Board, email, September 14, 2014)

This exemption meant that the administration of the surveys and focus groups had been determined by the IRB to pose a minimal risk to human welfare—however, the Library still had to "adhere to principles of sound research design and ethics" and protect "participant rights and welfare . . . in a manner appropriate for research that poses minimal risk" (University of Utah, n.d.).

The consultants were tasked with writing the survey questions, taking into account feedback from the dean and associate deans. Before distributing the resulting survey to the campus community, an electronic pre-survey was sent to ten Library employees to test the questions and ensure that the survey was ready for implementation. Both the pre-survey and the final survey were administered using SurveyMonkey, a free online survey tool.

Pre-survey participants were informed that the survey would take twenty to twenty-five minutes to complete, and that their input was needed in several areas:

- Do the survey questions make sense as they are currently phrased?

- Is the SurveyMonkey survey structure set up correctly (e.g., do the skip patterns work)?
- Are there any other operational issues with the instrument (e.g., response buttons not working properly, etc.)?
- How long does it take to complete the survey?

The Library employees were asked to complete the survey and send feedback directly to the consultants via email. In their feedback, participants were asked to list questions or concerns about the specific survey questions, as well as any general questions or comments about the survey's structure (appendix F).

Responses to the pre-survey were very helpful. They pointed out technical glitches and some instances of confusing phrasing, library jargon, and question duplication. The consultants then worked with Library administration to make needed changes, after which the final version of the survey was distributed to campus. The final survey (appendix G) was distributed via email and included a consent to participate that outlined the respondent's rights and responsibilities (appendix H).

The survey was made available to the entire campus community for a period of three weeks. A total of 3,232 responses were received. Out of those, 2,579 came from students, 483 from staff, 144 from faculty, and 24 from administrators (A breakdown of respondents by student level can be found in appendix I.) Participants included 107 library employees; 48 staff, 30 faculty, 12 student employees, and 8 library managers (as well as 9 respondents who classified themselves as "other"). Full results of the survey can be found in the final report (appendix I).

Just prior to the survey's distribution, a series of focus groups meetings began. Eight focus group sessions were held; the groups consisted of:

- Library faculty
- Library classified staff
- University administrators
- University academic faculty
- University classified staff
- Undergraduate and graduate students
- Library Executive Council members
- Library Strategic Planning Task Force members.

Each session lasted ninety minutes. In total, approximately ninety individuals from across campus participated. All sessions except for the one for students were conducted by the consultants. The Library's staff planning officer conducted focus group sessions for the students due to time constraints. Library administration had requested that the consultants increase the number of focus groups conducted from the time the contract was written to its implementation. This allowed the Library to reach a larger number of stakeholders but also meant that the consultants did not have enough time to conduct the student sessions. Conducting the students focus sessions fell to Library staff, increasing their workloads.

The objectives for these focus group sessions varied slightly from group to group but included discussions around the Library's past and present environment as well as recommendations for future changes to the Library's physical spaces and layout. Group discussion guides that included the questions to be addressed in each session were prepared by the consultants and were approved by the Library's administration and the university's IRB. The guides were distributed to the participants a few days prior to focus group meetings to allow them time to consider the questions, thus increasing the likelihood of receiving well-thought-out and useful feedback. Appendix J lists the questions asked of the focus groups.

Feedback revealed eleven areas of concern for future planning and development. These areas became target topics for the final draft of a strategic plan. These areas of concern included:

- library space
- infrastructure and technology
- technical capacity
- key obstacles in doing research/jobs/studies
- collection issues
- online collection and systems concerns
- help provided to users
- library advocacy/awareness/marketing
- library and university philosophies
- leadership
- workplace issues

The consultants synthesized all the data and information gathered from the focus groups and the survey and presented it at a meeting of Library employees. This information was further condensed into the final report (appendix I) for the Library's administration.

Lessons Learned

One of the first lessons learned during this process was that it takes longer to develop and field-test a survey than one might expect. Because the survey had been advertised for distribution on a specific date, there was no time to test it further after changes were made to the original one. In addition, there was not time to field test the survey to those outside the Library. Thankfully, the survey went well and had no major glitches, but it would have benefitted from being reviewed by informants from outside the Library and, additionally, a second field test would have been optimal.

Interestingly, one of the most difficult aspects of the survey process was unanticipated. The university had recently changed its approach to university-wide surveys and actively discouraged anyone from using mass email messages. Because mass emails were no longer an option for distributing the survey link, the Library's Public Relations and Marketing Director placed information about the survey in *@theU*, the university's weekly online newspaper.

A positive lesson learned (or more accurately, reinforced) was that incentives do work. To encourage student feedback on the survey, the Library held "tabling" events that offered students a chance to complete the survey right at a staffed table, and in return the student received a full-size candy bar—and whether they responded at a tabling event or remotely online, all students who completed the survey were entered into a drawing for an Xbox One, PlayStation4, Apple iPad Air, or GoPro HER03. The Library found that students responded enthusiastically to these incentives.

One important note is that, when using prizes as an incentive, make sure to check tax codes, especially at public higher education institutions where prizes may be considered taxable. All recipients of gifts were required to sign a gift acceptance letter (appendix K) to remain in compliance with federal regulations.

The focus groups elicited interesting information, but their cost-benefit ratio was high because they were time-consuming and, with only ninety attendees, may not have been as fully representative of campus attitudes as the Library would have wished. It was difficult to get people to commit to attending focus groups, even though a number of prospective attendees received individualized invitations.

To increase participation in the focus groups, the Library could have offered additional incentives for participation, especially to students who attended, just as the Library did for students who took the survey. Such incentives may have increased the number of focus group participants. In addition, because so few people attended, too much weight may have been given to the feedback received during the focus groups.

All in all, however, the surveys and the focus groups provided valuable insight into campus attitudes toward the Library and revealed the needs and expectations of users. This significantly helped the Library to shape its strategic plan.

4

Communication

CHAPTER 3 DISCUSSED METHODS OF GATHERING FEEDBACK and input from the library's various stakeholders in the beginning stages of the strategic planning process. This chapter will consider the importance of communicating *to* stakeholders—both during the planning process and (importantly) after the plan has been created. In a corporate context this practice would be called marketing.

Keeping stakeholders regularly and consistently updated on progress is an essential part of the strategic planning process. Different stakeholder groups may want different kinds of updates at various points in the planning timeline. For example, constituents outside the library may want infrequent updates or may only want access to final reports or the final strategic planning document itself, whereas library employees will likely want to have frequent updates with opportunities to give feedback at each stage.

Whatever method of facilitation (library, campus, or external) is chosen for the strategic planning process, it is important to clarify everyone's role in communicating discussion topics, decisions, and action items arising from each meeting with the various stakeholder groups. It is important to:

- Create a timeline to indicate when drafts of relevant documents will be available for library employees to consider and provide a mechanism to allow them to respond to those documents where appropriate.

- Be clear about what kinds of feedback are requested, what each should accomplish, and how the information will be used.
- Consider whether the same information will be given to all campus stakeholders or if the reporting will be kept to only a select few outside the library, for example, the provost, library board members, or others who have been heavily invested in the strategic planning process.

Many experts in change management, systems thinking, and organizational psychology recommend an abundance of communication during a change process. They often do not discuss the details of this communication, leaving many in leadership positions wondering what kinds of communication are needed and how much is enough. Unfortunately, there is not a simple or even a single answer to this question; the appropriate kinds and amount of external communication must be determined in light of the library's particular situation. Factors that should be taken into consideration include:

- How large is the faculty and student body? (They form the library's primary stakeholder group, and the larger it is, the less possible it will be to communicate with individuals or small groups. External communication will need to be tailored for large sub-populations of the group; the smaller is the group, the more flexibility will be possible.)
- What kinds of changes to library structure and service are being contemplated? (The more radical the possible changes, the more important it will be to give stakeholders advance notice and perhaps additional opportunities to provide feedback.)
- How surprising does the library believe its stakeholders will find its change(s) in direction? (The more unexpected the changes are likely to be, the more important it is to give stakeholders ample time to prepare for them.)

The library should be careful not to rush the communication process unduly during the strategic planning process. Although there is no need to delay or dawdle through that process, it is also important not to be overly hasty—a day or two saved by shortcutting communication may result in unintended consequences that require more time (and work) later. It is also important to remember that employees themselves are an essential part of the library's stakeholder group. Jick (2009) encouraged taking time to gather and incorporate feedback, particularly from employees, stating that, "It is a fundamental tenet of participative management that employees are more likely to support what they help create . . . it is difficult to *get* cooperation, negotiation, and compromise from people who are effectively ordered to change, never listened to or supported" (415).

Once the strategic plan is finalized and the resulting changes have been put in motion, the need for external communication does not end. It is important to widely communicate the plan across campus, perhaps in multiple versions: a brief summary for broadest distribution, an outline document with more detail for those closer to the library, and a fully-detailed report for those with the deepest interest and closest connections. Apart from the importance of such reports in communicating the details of the new strategic plan, they can also be a great way to draw attention to the library's key services and resources.

THE MARRIOTT LIBRARY'S STORY

Communication

The Marriott Library's strategic plan represented an effort to create a five-year pathway to its desired goals, one that was explicitly aligned to the university's strategic goals. Successfully engaging Library faculty and staff, as well as the university community and administration, required the Library to create a solid and creative marketing program that included full use of social networking in addition to more traditional marketing techniques. The plan had to be both *understood* and *recognized as legitimate* by internal and external stakeholders.

From the beginning of the strategic planning process, the EC addressed the need for marketing both the process (development of the plan) and implementation of the plan itself. Germano and Stretch-Stephenson (2012) emphasized the importance of looking at "current trends in market planning, especially those aimed at utilizing the marketing function as a critical element of strategic planning and execution" (71). They also concluded that "when market-driven value is infused into the strategic planning processes while at the same time being bolstered by a subsequent post-planning selling effort in order to ensure that internal and external stakeholders buy into and value the strategic planning goals, there is greater likelihood of a successful outcome" (85). Because of just such considerations, the EC felt it important to have a name for the plan, and thus it was dubbed "Imagine U: Creating YOUR Library of the Future," a title that referred deliberately and specifically to the University of Utah's recently adopted slogan "Imagine U."

Internally, the Library sought to balance a desire for transparency (tell everyone everything all the time) with the need to avoid unnecessary distress or information overload. In pursuit of that balance, the Library made sure to provide time for sharing strategic planning drafts with staff, gathering employee feedback, acknowledging all feedback while incorporating as much as was deemed reasonable, and reporting about those changes that grew out of the feedback. Throughout the process, Library leaders emphasized that although all feedback would be heard and given full consideration, it would be impossible to incorporate all of it—and encouraged staff to bear in mind that just because a particular piece of counsel or advice was not adopted did not mean it had not been heard or considered. This can be difficult for staff to understand. It is human nature to assume that if one's ideas are not fully embraced and made actionable, they have not been fully considered. Being transparent from the very beginning of the process can prove helpful, but it does not solve this problem. It will need to be addressed throughout the strategic planning process.

During the strategic planning process, the Marriott Library engaged the campus and Library in several ways, including:

> Inviting campus, community, and Library employees to share observations about where the Library was succeeding and what needed to be added or addressed.
>
> Sharing regular but infrequent interim reports and final strategic directions with campus administration.
>
> Meeting one-on-one with those employees most affected by proposed organizational changes. Most people do not like to be surprised in a group setting with important information that will impact their jobs, and they appreciate the respect demonstrated by meeting face-to-face.
>
> Inviting feedback on a draft version of the final strategic plan at an all-staff meeting. Feedback from that meeting led the Library to change from calling the document a "strategic plan" to characterizing it as a list of "strategic directions." Staff feedback also had a significant impact on the overall look of the final product, adding new images and a different layout.

It is also essential to bear in mind that communication, one of the most important aspects of any strategic planning effort, does not end with the conclusion of the strategic planning process itself. In the Marriott Library, communication has continued with Library employees in a number of different manifestations and venues:

> Library employees are invited to a monthly coffee-and-cookies gathering with one of the associate deans or the dean. The agenda for the conversation is set by the employees.
>
> The dean meets with all employees annually (in small groups) for an open conversation.
>
> EC decisions and action items are shared with all Library employees.

Although staff have an annual review, a six-month check-in process was implemented for employees. It offers an opportunity to assess if employees feel valued and part of the Library community and if they have the tools and training they need to be successful.

A new standing Library Services Committee was formed, with representation from all Library divisions, creating more buy-in across the Library for new, changed, or removed services.

A new Library intranet was implemented that allows for easy sharing of documents, information, work flows, and progress. It is used:

- to manage communication and collaboration and serve as the official repository for policies, forms, and internal documents
- as the place where Library teams and individuals create, manage, and store information that they use to collaborate with each other and on their projects
- to encourage communication and collaborative work across departmental lines
- to foster organizational knowledge and citizenship
- to share news and information about library services to engage and motivate employees and support the delivery of library services
- to collaborate on document creation and engagement with internal closed groups
- to provide individual file storage and access

Lessons Learned

Although the Library administration worked diligently to maintain an open dialog and transparent communication, more communication, or maybe different communication, or perhaps both—more and different—was needed.

In retrospect, it would have been helpful to provide staff with more frequent updates, such as consistent weekly messages that clearly spelled out what was occurring, that is, not just updates about what had already taken place, but also information about what was in the process of being implemented, to provide an opportunity for staff to weigh in on those implementations *prior* to their occurrence. The intranet mechanism that the Library put in place turned out to be clunky and difficult to use both for placing messages and for finding and accessing information. A new intranet platform was put in place partly because of the problems that occurred during the strategic planning process and offers more robust communication options.

As libraries consider strategic planning, the authors strongly suggest that robust internal communication systems be installed and tested as one of the first steps in the process. It is also important that at the very beginning of the planning process, a communication plan be established that clearly outlines a timeline of regular updates and opportunities for input prior to implementation and serves as a mechanism for timely responses to feedback.

Establishing and maintaining communication with campus and other stakeholders is important before, during, and after the strategic planning process. Although the Library gathered information before and during the planning process, once the final report had been presented to campus, few updates or opportunities for feedback specific to how the strategic plan is progressing were extended to campus or external stakeholders. This was a missed opportunity to not only assess the strategic plan but to also maintain contact with stakeholders.

The Library's next strategic planning initiative is nearing. Communication will be a major topic of concern. Although a robust internal communication system is now in place, the Library plans to consider ways to connect with campus and other stakeholders to get their feedback during all aspects of the planning process and then to engage with them on an ongoing basis after a new strategic plan is in place.

5

Implementation

ONE OF THE MORE IMPORTANT, AND POTENTIALLY DISRUPTIVE, impacts that strategic planning can have is a change in organizational structure. Once the strategic plan has been finalized, an important question the library should ask itself is whether the current organizational structure will help the library achieve the strategic goals it has just identified, or if it will be an impediment. In discussing the importance of structure in an organization, Bolman and Deal (2013, 46) suggested that organizational structure "is a blueprint for formal expectations and exchanges among internal players (managers, executives, employees) and external constituencies (such as customers and clients)." Formal structure can have a positive or negative impact on the organization depending on whether it enhances morale or impedes progress. (For the purposes of this book, the authors use the terms "restructure" and "reorganize" interchangeably, both being intended to mean "bring about change within the organization by adjusting reporting lines, departmental boundaries, and/or the allocation of tasks to individuals and groups.")

Bolman and Deal (2013, 84) laid out a variety of reasons for organizational restructuring, including:

- the environment shifts
- technology changes

- organizations grow
- leadership changes

In the specific context of academic libraries, Nutefall and Chadwell (2012, 171) suggested that "there are many valid or worthwhile reasons why an academic library might elect to undergo a realignment process: tremendous technological change, severe budgetary need, or evolving management or change theory." Chan and Soong (2011, 27) found that in the case of their own library, reorganization was undertaken to "reposition the Library strategically and realign [the library's] resources so that it can continue to provide users with best services in the coming years, in spite of staffing and funding constraints."

Meier (2016, 264), on the other hand, began his study with the hypothesis that, in libraries, "organizational change is primarily driven by financial constraints and personnel changes rather than strategic initiatives." However, subsequent interviews with library leaders during the course of his investigation led him to conclude that "organizational decisions and shifts appear to follow strategic planning" (282). In fact, 59 percent of the respondents to Meier's survey question "How will your strategic plan and vision affect the organization of your library?" chose the response: "strategic plan drives organizational structure" (272). Thus, although it would not be accurate to make a blanket assertion that reorganization always follows strategic planning, it seems to be a common outcome.

Reorganization can take any number of forms, some of them relatively minor and others deep and far-reaching. Moving a single or a few individual employees between departments or formulating different duties within a unit are examples of smaller and less-disruptive restructuring. On the other hand, creating entirely new organizational units for the purpose of developing new services, or even eliminating entire departments when their roles are decreasing in importance, are examples of highly disruptive and potentially traumatic organizational change. The deeper and more far-reaching a reorganization effort is, the more time-consuming and stressful it will be for everyone in the organization—and the more directly employees are impacted, the more difficult it will be for them. Chan and Soong (2016, 27) asserted, "Making substantial adjustments or changes to existing organizational structure are not simple tasks, as they often generate anxiety and unrest among staff as well as causing confusion to users." Heidari-Robinson and Heywood (2016, 2) weighed in, "Research suggests that reorgs—and the uncertainty they provoke about the future—can cause greater stress and anxiety than layoffs, leading in about 60% of cases to noticeably reduced productivity."

Although reorganization is disruptive and stressful, and change for the sake of change is never a good idea, academic libraries cannot afford to remain static when change is truly needed in order for the library to remain mission-critical to its host institution. Bolman and Deal (2013, 85) suggested that "because a stable structure reduces confusion and uncertainty, maintains internal consistency, and protects the existing equilibrium," organizations may hesitate to make significant structural changes. However, the authors also pointed out that "the price of stability is a structure that grows increasingly misaligned with the environment. Eventually, the gap gets so big that a major overhaul is inevitable" (85).

With major changes in technology and in users' needs and expectations, along with the evolving needs and challenges of higher education, academic libraries that do not make careful and strategic adjustments will eventually be left behind and may find it more difficult to prove their worth to their users, university administrators, and external funders. Chan and Soong (2011, 27) concurred: "As our environment continues to change, we not only need to continue to improve our library services and enhance our service facilities, but also need to adjust our service strategies and ways of thinking and streamline our operations and procedures."

THE MARRIOTT LIBRARY'S STORY

Implementation and Reorganization

The document entitled *Strategic Directions 2015–2020* (appendix D) became the basis of a Library-wide reorganization. The reorganization was based on needs and priorities that were identified or clarified through the strategic planning process. Although the Library had many talented, dedicated employees, it was not organizationally structured to meet the quickly evolving needs of today's students, researchers, and faculty. Too many Library staff and faculty were allocated to areas of decreasing strategic importance (e.g., cataloging print books), while areas of growing importance (e.g., digital initiatives), had a shortage of staff. Also, some similar work functions were spread across different departments, causing waste and duplication of effort. The Library realized that to meet the needs of users and expectations of the campus community, staffing needed to be reconfigured. The Library's existing four divisions, as well as its administrative units, were reorganized.

The following list of organizational changes indicates how different areas were strengthened, disbanded, reduced, combined, or shifted.

Special Collections Division
- reassigned four faculty positions to Book Arts from other areas
- converted three part-time temporary staff positions into full-time permanent positions and assigned them to various departments
- began managing the Preservation Unit (which had been part of the Collections and Scholarly Resources division)
- moved the Middle East department from Special Collections to Research and User Services division

Collections and Scholarly Communication Division

- created the Scholarly Communication department
- dissolved the Cataloging and Metadata Services department, eliminating some vacant positions and distributing catalogers to other areas in the Library

Research and User Services Division

- consolidated two service desks, reassigning student salaries for use elsewhere in the Library
- redirected Library faculty from service desks to allow an increased focus on research and teaching efforts and deployed staff to provide assistance at service desks
- created a new department (Creativity and Innovation Services) to work with students on technology and creative projects in a "neutral" space
- absorbed the Middle East Library unit (which had been part of the Special Collections Division)
- piloted a project that placed a librarian on site at the Utah Asia Campus

Information Technology and Digital Library Services Division

- merged eight existing IT departments/units into three departments, with similarly functional units grouped together
- combined Digital Operations, Digital Preservation, and part of Cataloging and Metadata Services into one new department (Digital Library Services) to create, access, and preserve digital assets, eliminating redundancies
- created a Digital Infrastructure department that was charged with supporting technology needs for digital projects across the Library, including Digital Library Services
- combined Windows and Mac support groups into one department to shift focus from specific technology platforms to user-centered services
- reassigned a vacant faculty position to work with data management

Library Administration

- reassigned two vacant staff positions to the Development unit
- reassigned one vacant staff position to the PR and Marketing Unit
- reassigned a vacant position (receptionist in Administrative Offices) to create an Events and Scheduler Coordinator position
- increased Grants Administrator duties to include Library assessment
- created the Budget Advisory Committee, made up of staff and faculty, to offer feedback to the Dean

Three entirely new departments were created under the reorganization: Creativity and Innovation Services, Digital Library Services, and Scholarly Communications. Additionally, a new initiative, Digital Matters Lab, was added in 2016.

Creativity and Innovation Services
(Research and User Services Division)

Several disparate Library units were brought together to form Creativity and Innovation Services to offer users collaborative support and expertise in arts and design, media production, visual communication, fabrication technology, and interactive media.

Digital Library Services
(Information Technology and Digital Library Services Division)

Before the reorganization, digitization work was spread across multiple departments, making it difficult for users to know where to go for different services. Reorganization brought all digitization projects into one newly created department, Digital Library Services (DLS), which provides online access to unique primary source materials, assists with research and teaching, and helps faculty convert analog manuscripts or objects into digital formats to include in publications. DLS is responsible for all digitization, metadata, and digital preservation within the Library and collaborates with the university's colleges and units, as well as with other groups in Utah.

Scholarly Communications
(Collections and Scholarly Communications Division)

Recent developments in the realm of scholarly and scientific publishing have made that landscape much more complex. The emergence and proliferation of open access models, alternatives to traditional copyright, institutional repositories, predatory and deceptive publishing operations, and new forms of publishing (including the growing phenomenon of preprint servers) led the Library to establish this department charged with monitoring developments in scholarly communication and to offer services to faculty and students that will help them navigate that constantly-shifting landscape.

Digital Matters Lab
(Research and User Services Division)

The Digital Matters Lab is a collaborative venture of the Library and the Colleges of Humanities, Architecture and Planning, and Fine Arts. The lab provides the space, tools, and expertise necessary for computationally enhanced research and teaching. It serves as a hub of innovation and a center for dynamic partnership across campus.

The reorganization affected almost every employee. As part of the reorganization effort, Library administration invited the university Counseling Center staff to speak to employees at all-staff meeting about managing change and specific "Coaching through Change" training was also offered. In addition, employees were encouraged to give feedback on the reorganization efforts through group meetings as well as one-on-one meetings with the dean and associate deans.

Lessons Learned

As all major projects do, the Library's strategic planning process created learning opportunities for the organization. One such opportunity came between the time that the Library proposed its new organizational structure and the implementation of this reorganization. Although one-on-one meetings were held between cognizant associate deans and those who would be personally affected by the changes, there was not enough time to consider feedback from the staff and discern what adjustments should have been addressed in light of those concerns.

Some of the most difficult tasks in a reorganization are listening to feedback, acting on that feedback when it is prudent to do so, and helping staff understand why some feedback will not be acted upon. Library administrators made it clear from the beginning of the strategic planning process that staff feedback would be listened to and addressed, but this would not mean all feedback would be implemented. However, given more time, some feedback might have gained more traction. For example, as part of the reorganization, a few names of departments and divisions were changed. One division, formerly called "Research and Learning Services," had its name changed to "Graduate and Undergraduate Services." This change was met with great resistance from library faculty because of the absence of any language regarding teaching, instruction, learning, or education. Following the language of the campus goals, this same language had been removed from the Library's goals, with teaching and learning being subsumed under the goal "Promote student success to transform lives." In the minds of Library administration, this meant the same thing as teaching students to be more information-literate. In the minds of Library faculty, this was an example of what Jick said can happen when "those seeking to produce change fail to understand or identify with the core values of the system they seek to influence" (2008, 413). These employees were certain that the Library administration no longer valued the education functions performed by Library faculty. One of the important lessons learned from this process was that it is important to pay close attention to staff resistance that may reveal perceptions of diminished status.

Of course, it is never possible to make everyone happy, and at a certain point the organization had to move from "selling to telling." After listening carefully to feedback and incorporating some changes, the period allotted for negotiations ended, and it was time to announce the final decision. Library leaders had to be clear during this part of the process so that employees knew when the time for negotiation had ended but could also feel confident that their concerns had been heard, and understood that although some adjustments would be made in response to their suggestions, not all suggestions could be undertaken.

Was a reorganization needed after the drafting of the strategic plan? The authors believe that a reorganization was warranted to successfully align the Library with the university's strategic goals. Did this many radical changes need to be made at the same time, or would incremental changes have been easier for the staff and have been equally effective? Because this was not the approach taken, the authors can only speculate that it might have been easier in the short term but overall do not feel that incremental change would have been easier on the staff or that it would have created a more effective outcome.

6

Assessment

A S DESCRIBED IN EARLIER CHAPTERS, WRITING A STRATEGIC plan is labor-intensive and costly in terms of both staff time and resources. Once the strategic plan has been written, it might be tempting to think the hard work is over, but the most important part is only beginning; after all, a completed strategic plan is only valuable to the degree that it is successfully implemented and thereby brings about desired change. Once the plan has been written, implementation begins, and with it comes questions that will need to be regularly reviewed and answered. These include:

- Is the library using the strategic plan in its regular and short-term planning and program development?
- Are the goals that are outlined in the strategic plan reflected in the day-to-day work of the library?
- Is the library making steady progress toward the realization of the specific goals laid out in the strategic plan?
- Are the strategic goals still valid as each year passes? If not, what adjustments are needed? (Remember that a strategic plan should not be a dead document, but a flexible and living program that can adjust to changes in the environment.)

Asking such questions is part of an ongoing assessment strategy. Assessment of strategic plans is discussed in the literature, including McNicol's (2005) article in which library directors in several UK institutions of higher education were interviewed about their involvement in their institutions' planning processes. One director noted that the "library is good at counting things, e.g., number of loans, but has not really done anything to see the value of those things" (505). Germano and Stretch-Stephenson (2012, 73) argued that "success is further predicated upon value creation that allows the library to achieve measurable, value-oriented goals as part of the plan's execution whether they are related to fundraising, succession planning or something as straightforward as increased use of the library." Assessment then is not just about "counting things" but also involves asking the question, "What is the value in what the library does?" For example, if one of the library's strategic goals is "student success," the library might routinely ask itself several questions in relation to this goal:

- Is it still a valid goal for the library as each year passes?
- What is the library doing to ensure student success?
- How are the library's activities moving it closer to achieving that goal?
- Are any of the library's activities undermining its ability to achieve that goal?

Even if it is agreed upon that assessment means more than "counting things," this does not mean that things do not need to be counted. It only means that the counting of things should always have a strategic purpose when it comes to assessment. For example, if more electronic journal articles are being downloaded this year than last year, what impact, if any, has that increase had for student success? How can that impact be demonstrated?

THE MARRIOTT LIBRARY'S STORY

Assessment

The Marriott Library adopted a plan that was different from typical strategic plans in that it listed strategic "directions" rather than "goals." The difference between strategic "directions" versus "goals" is that strategic directions outline a path to follow, but do not insist on a specific path to attain success. For example, the first strategic direction the Library adopted was "Promote Student Success to Transform Lives." Although under that strategic direction are two specific points, "Creatively use resources and space to meet campus needs" and "Provide seamless and responsive assistance for students," by contrast, a strategic goal would have more specific outcomes such as "increasing the number of students taught by 30% by 2020."

Using a less specific aim allowed employees to develop multiple avenues to move in this direction without dictating only one way to succeed. This encouraged employees to ask how their work was aligned with the direction and provided them with the responsibility of defining ways to lead the Library that connected with the strategic direction.

Another way the Library proceeded down a different path was the incorporation of assessment into the implementation of the Strategic Directions. Although beginning with the first leadership retreat the EC emphasized the need for assessment to show progress in the strategic directions, because the final set of strategic directions was different from a typical strategic plan with specific goals, the assessment process has taken a unique approach.

The process of assessment began first when the dean assigned two people to take charge of each of the six strategic directions as facilitators. With six strategic directions, the plan was to have a total of twelve facilitators. One additional facilitator was added to the group due to personnel changes, for a total of thirteen. The facilitators included the four associate deans, four directors, three staff members, and two faculty librarians.

Recognizing that accountability would be an important element in measuring success, facilitators gathered information from around the Library regarding the progress of employees in contributing to their assigned strategic direction. In addition, some facilitators oversaw the work toward implementing a strategic direction simply because the new idea was within their line of responsibility. Every six months during the first two years, and annually thereafter, at one of the Library's monthly all-staff meetings, the facilitators gave presentations on accomplishments and progress across the organization.

To gather data for these assessment presentations, each pair of facilitators held open discussions with Library employees to discuss the particular strategic direction assigned to them, and to assess progress in that direction. The facilitators invited participants to speak with them about information or statistics that could be collected, about future plans, and about potential pilot projects. The facilitators encouraged the group to keep track of early successes, to report on roadblocks, and to consider whether there might be services or programs the Library should consider stopping.

Initially, these open discussions created more questions than answers. For example, as the two facilitators charged with overseeing "Promote Student Success to Transform Lives" discussed that direction at an open forum, questions arose such as:

- What type of student space is needed?
- What additional signage and marketing are needed to increase awareness of the spaces already available?
- How does the library create temporary group study areas to meet the increasing student demand?
- How can the Library better accommodate student needs?

This brainstorming often led to specific changes, as suggested by library employees. For example, the head of the Graduate and Undergraduate Services department participated in discussions for the strategic direction, "Promote Student Success to Transform Lives." This department head realized that the Library was putting strong emphasis on the success of undergraduate students but paying less attention to that of graduate students. She approached one of the facilitators with a plan to strengthen graduate student services, and thereby to "Promote (Graduate) Student Success."

Even as these open discussions led to improvements in programs and services, Library employees also began to ask the question, "what can we stop doing?" Increasing efforts in one area required balancing efforts in others to avoid the typical burnout that can take place without this balance. As the result of a newly accepted faculty charter, new committees were formed that superseded the Library's prior committee structure: thus, for example, what had been the Outreach and User Services Council was terminated and replaced with the Library Services Committee. Other committees were also disbanded as new organizational structures and leadership formed in response to the new strategic plan.

Library services and spaces came under the spotlight of assessment as employees took to heart the desire to "Promote Student Success," "Develop and Transfer New Knowledge," and "Promote a Healthy Learning and Work Environment." A task force was created to review the four service points available on the second floor of the Library and those service points were reduced to two in 2016 and then to one in 2018. An evaluation of reference services, both in person and online, resulted in a reduction in the involvement of librarians on the service desk, and led to an increase in the number of staff hired to organize and manage these service points—this eventually led to student employees being trained to manage the Library's online chat reference service. This provided additional time for librarians to focus on outreach to faculty and students along with their research and creative activity.

These changes created a continual need to evaluate and review the organizational chart. After the initial major reorganization, minor adjustments continue each year. These organizational changes led to salary equity studies across the organization and a plan to improve salaries for all employees. Improvement of pay for employees was the number one issue discussed at the "Enhance Library Employee Potential," goal six, open forums. Although all salary problems could not be solved at once, each year a different subset of the most urgent salary issues is addressed.

Assessment of the strategic direction "Develop and Transfer New Knowledge," goal two, led to two significant changes: an increased focus on librarian productivity in research and the creation of a research hub facilitating digital scholarship across campus. In the past, research and creative activity had not been an area of significant focus for librarians, but the university's administration had a renewed emphasis on faculty research and publication. The creation of this strategic direction and a newly-adopted set of criteria for review and promotion of library faculty breathed new life into this effort. Additionally, one of the notable descriptions of the strategic direction, "Enhance Library Employee Potential," was the development of a mentoring program that began with the purpose of helping faculty with their research and creative output.

The renewed focus on scholarly output created an opportunity to strengthen the assessment methodology as faculty and staff began to ask the question, "how do I know if this new service, space, furniture, advertising, etc. worked?" New research projects began to emerge and collaborations between faculty and staff were highlighted in articles and presentations. A formal plan for research support in the form of retreats, workshops, additional funding for travel, writing groups, and outside speakers formed the basis of a faculty mentoring program.

As these changes were implemented, a new tension came into focus, one related to the use of Library space. The Library needed more classroom space, group study spaces, space for research, and space for the collections. Multiple construction projects were underway on campus, most of them beginning with the elimination of classrooms in buildings that were being replaced. In each case, this loss of classroom space led to increased pressure on Library classrooms as departments looked to the Library to help ease the pressure on their instructors. As the Library attempted to move in new strategic directions, staff engaged in a constant effort to balance the internal needs of the Library with those of the campus.

At the same time, discussions with campus faculty had made clear their desire that the Library maintain a robust collection of printed materials on site, and their concern about the prospect of withdrawals—even of items held widely in other libraries and that were seldom (or never) used in the Marriott Library. In pursuit of the strategic direction "Ensure Long-Term Viability of the U," goal three, the Library approached donors with an invitation to help the Library realize its vision of designing spaces for all constituents while maintaining a robust circulating collection within the building. The result was an increase in donations that allowed the Library to purchase and install compact shelving, create classroom space, and open a space for a research hub.

The question of the need for a research hub had initially arisen during assessment discussions around the strategic direction "Develop and Transfer New Knowledge." Library staff wondered whether there was an expressed need on campus for a new program such as this, and initially the answer seemed to be "no." Over the course of a year, however, three different colleges (Humanities, Fine Arts, and Architecture + Planning) approached the Library with a specific need for a central, neutral space for conducting digitally-enhanced research and creative activity. These initial discussions led to the creation of the Digital Matters Lab, the establishment of which was supported by an anonymous donation sufficient to hire a director and support programming for five years.

In addition, an informal assessment committee was created with faculty and staff participants to review all data collected to make sure that unnecessary data-collection activities would be eliminated. This group initiated a campus-wide assessment of the Library four years after the implementation of the strategic plan to further enhance assessment efforts. As these changes and improvements were discussed annually at all-staff meetings, a Library-wide culture of assessment and progress began to take hold.

Lessons Learned

Since specific people were assigned to oversee pursuit of the strategic directions throughout the life of the plan, there has been some reduction of excitement about the strategic directions among those not assigned specifically to oversee them, and as these directions have become commonplace and been incorporated into everyone's daily work. In retrospect, it might have been better to create a different oversight structure, perhaps with three employees for each direction, one of them being replaced each year as a facilitator to bring diversity of thought and new excitement to the ongoing assessment process. Because there has been some degree of inevitable turnover in personnel during the five-year life of our plan, instituting a deliberate program of change among the facilitators would have made sense in any case.

As the end of the time frame laid out for these strategic directions quickly approaches, gathering information about the Library's progress will be difficult without a common space for the collection of the annual presentations, statistics, and accomplishments. In retrospect, it would have been wise to establish a formal data management plan at the outset, one that would have laid out a strategy for collecting and curating all such information. The implementation of a new library intranet will facilitate the process of data collection in the future and for the next round of strategic planning.

On the positive side, the Library discovered that inviting everyone to participate in the interpretation of the strategic directions and in the ongoing assessment process has repeatedly led to new discoveries and staff-led initiatives. Areas of campus research and teaching are more easily addressed with the opportunity for employees to come together around specific strategic directions. Reviewing the Library's strengths and weaknesses has led to the strengthening of programs and services that had previously been neglected. And seriously considering what programs and practices could be stopped has led to innovative ideas and the rearrangement of spaces and staffing to better serve library constituents.

Inviting all library employees to engage in the process of evaluation is precisely what is recommended by Oshry (1992) in his book *The Possibilities of Organization*. Oshry (1992, 158) encourages leaders to "create conditions that make it possible for [employees] to be responsible" for the success of the organization. One way to accomplish that task is to "involve others in the big issues" facing top leadership (159). Asking for help with high-level strategic directions fostered a culture of Library-wide responsibility for strategic success on the part of employees. When leadership followed this advice, it also reduced the likelihood of "internal warfare" that naturally occurs whenever people form an organization (28). According to Oshry, by allowing employees to take responsibility, the Library opens "possibilities for greater accomplishment, for more satisfying and more productive relationships and for higher quality service to the Customer" (104).

Assessment can and should be more than just counting things. Allowing for a more informal, free flow of ideas and concerns encourages employees to create inventive ways to overcome obstacles and envision better paths to the Library's strategic goals. Keeping track of changes, improvements, and data is essential for sustaining organizational energy around those strategic directions.

7

Tying It All Together

THROUGHOUT THIS BOOK THE AUTHORS HAVE COMBINED A DIS-
cussion of general principles of strategic planning with real-world illustrations of these principles drawn from the lived experience of strategic planning
at the J. Willard Marriott Library at the University of Utah. This final chapter
pulls the core principles together and presents a summary statement of the
essential elements of a successful planning process, along with a few additional ideas in connection with each of them.

"Why," Then "How"

As with most major undertakings, effective strategic planning begins not with
the question "How shall we do it?" but rather with the question "Why do we
believe we should do this?"—and its corollary question, "What problem are
we trying to solve?"

A strategic plan is something that many organizations simply assume
they ought to have, but given the tremendous cost in terms of both time and
money that the planning process will necessarily entail, "Because we ought

to have one" is simply not a sufficient answer to the question "Why are we creating a strategic plan?"

The authors suggest two key questions that can be particularly helpful to consider as the library is preparing to undertake this project.

The first is *What do we hope to achieve with our strategic plan?* Presumably, the impulse to engage in a planning project is being prompted by something— perhaps the library's organizational structure is beginning to feel unbalanced, or its programs are drifting out of alignment with the needs of patrons and the host institution, or challenges are coming into view on the horizon for which the library does not seem well prepared. Whatever the issue or issues may be, bringing them into clear focus is an important first step before beginning the process of strategic planning.

The second question is *How will we know whether we have achieved it?* We will come back to the question of assessment later in this concluding chapter, but for now it is worth noting that although assessment happens primarily after the planning process has been completed, at the macro level it is both possible and desirable to have an idea from the very beginning as to how the library will recognize the success (or failure) of the strategic plan once the plan is in place. Will staff morale have markedly improved? Will the lines of communication between the library and university administration be clearer and more direct? Will there be noticeably greater alignment between the library's programs and the host institution's academic or research priorities? Some of these measures will be more quantifiable than others, but even in the case of those that are more qualitative, it will be important to have a general idea of how the library intends to assess the success of the planning project.

Overplanning Is Better Than Underplanning

Obviously, the ideal would be to plan neither too much nor too little, but rather to plan *just enough*. However, that balance is elusive, and the downside risk of underplanning is much greater than the cost of overplanning— so most libraries, when preparing to embark on a strategic planning project, should plan to overplan. It is also worth noting that there is a time and place for improvisation and spontaneity in the life of any organization, including libraries. But strategic planning will not usually be that time or that place.

In this book the authors have urged the reader to "plan to plan," meaning that it is important to create a framework ahead of time that will guide the strategic planning process itself. That framework should answer such questions as:

- What is the timeline for the planning process?
- Who has overall responsibility for the process?

- Who are the stakeholders?
- How and to what degree does the library intend to align its strategic plan to that of the host institution?

Perhaps the two most important of these questions are those that deal with identifying the library's stakeholders and determining the degree to which the library will seek to align its strategic plan with that of the host institution (or, in the absence of an institutional strategic plan, with the institution's expressed priorities). Regarding the latter, the authors have strongly urged readers to work toward just such institutional alignment.

Alignment, Alignment, Alignment

In fact, this may be the right point at which to emphasize the central importance of institutional alignment—both in the context of strategic planning and in the broader context of library planning, policy formation, and project management generally. Throughout the planning process it will be essential to keep in mind that the library's strategic goals are not being formulated in an organizational vacuum. The academic library is a unit of a larger institution, on which it depends for its support and to which it has obligations that include support of the institution's mission and goals. A failure to align the library's strategic goals with the priorities of its host institution will, eventually, but inevitably, lead to a loss of support from the institution—as, one could argue, it should.

Balancing Focus and Flexibility

Having just suggested that strategic planning will not usually be either the time or the place for spontaneity and improvisation, here it is important to offer an important caveat: no one (and no organization) can plan for every contingency. Thus, it is important to be prepared for the likelihood that unintended consequences and external events will impinge in unanticipated ways both on the strategic planning process and on the library after a strategic plan has been completed and put in place. For example, the university president may suddenly leave while the library is halfway through its planning process, leaving the university's strategic priorities for the next five years unclear; even worse, the president may depart shortly after the strategic plan has been completed, leaving the newly-completed plan's ongoing relevance uncertain to some degree. Or a budget crisis may suddenly constrict the library's options, rendering significant portions of the strategic plan moot, at least temporarily.

What all of this means is that although the strategic plan must be tightly and specifically conceived enough to be useful, it also must include room for adaptation in the inevitable event of unforeseen developments.

Prepare for Resistance and Fear

When one is in an administrative position in an academic library, it is very easy to lose sight of what working in that library is like for those on the front lines. It is important to bear in mind that although the prospect of strategic planning may be an exciting and invigorating (or even merely exhausting) one for the library leaders who will be in control of the process and will have final say in its ultimate outcomes, for those elsewhere in the organization—who will not be in control of the process and will not have final say in its outcomes—it may, quite reasonably, be seen as a threat: to the integrity of workflows that they have perfected over a number of years; to organizational structures in which they have learned how to function effectively; to priorities that they believe to be appropriate.

Here, however, it is essential for library leaders to bear in mind that resistance to change does not necessarily arise either from fear or from an aversion to change as such. It can be all too easy, when resistance is encountered, to dismiss it by saying "Well, everyone hates change so this is to be expected." Resistance can, and often does, arise not from an aversion to change itself, but from a considered evaluation of the particular changes being contemplated, and a feeling that they are not the right ones. This reality means that leaders need to listen very carefully when staff raise questions and concerns and avoid the temptation to dismiss them as mere reaction. Remember that staff who raise concerns are not the enemy; they are fellow employees who have a perspective on the workings of the library that is very different from that of administration—and that may be, in some ways at least, superior. For example, an administrator will likely have a better sense of budget realities, but facilities staff will likely have a better idea of how the study spaces in the library are being used by patrons.

When resistance and concerns are encountered, it may be important (not to mention tempting) to offer assurances, but at the same time it is essential to be honest and candid about what can and cannot be promised during the strategic planning process. The only thing library staff hate more than disruption is the promise of no disruption—followed by disruption. Promises that cannot be kept may dampen the fires of resistance temporarily, but those fires will roar back to life later when the promises are not kept.

Facilitators Are the Secret Sauce of Strategic Planning

Much of the success of the strategic planning process will depend on who facilitates it. The facilitators are the one constant element throughout the process, and their attitude and approach will color everything that happens during it. This means that the choice of facilitators will be one of the earliest and most consequential decisions administrators will make.

The authors have outlined multiple possible strategies for finding facilitators, but highly recommend that they be brought in from outside the library—and, if possible, from outside the academic institution. Although both internal and external facilitation will create challenges, the specific challenges that will arise from using internal facilitators are more serious and more likely to have a lasting negative impact. For example, one of the great benefits of bringing in outsiders to facilitate is that they will leave when the plan has been completed. This frees them to provide candid input throughout the planning process, without having to worry about fallout from their colleagues. Outside facilitators will also come to focus-group discussions without any of the institutional history, relationships, and baggage that library employees will inevitably have.

However, if the library does decide to bring in outside facilitators, it will be essential for the library's leadership to make clear to all parties—from the very beginning of the process—that they take full ownership of and responsibility for the final products of the strategic planning process. The content of the final version will be determined by library leadership, and mistakes (if any) should not be blamed on the outside facilitators.

Gather Feedback Early and Often

This may seem obvious, but it is important enough to be worth emphasizing: do not wait to gather feedback on the strategic plan until after the plan has been completed. The times to gather feedback are before, during, and after the process. In fact, gathering feedback, on the library's current services, practices, and policies as well as on ideas for future change, is an absolutely crucial element of the strategic planning process itself. This can be challenging because if the feedback-gathering is effective it will yield input that may be difficult or painful to hear. But that, of course, is exactly its purpose: an important function of strategic planning is that it generates comments that library leadership and staff may not want to hear. The pain felt in that moment is growing pain, the best kind of pain for any organization.

With this in mind, it will be essential for the library to think expansively, but critically, about the makeup of its stakeholder group, bearing in mind that although the library may serve a large and broad population, some subgroups of that population may have a greater claim on the library's staff, services, and collections than others do. The library at a public university, for example, may have an explicit, even statutory, obligation to serve the general public—but its primary obligation will be to the students and faculty of the university. This reality has implications both for library policy and for the ways in which the library will solicit and ingest feedback during the strategic planning process.

Communication with Stakeholders Is Not Just About Listening, but Also about Speaking

As important as it is to gather feedback throughout the strategic planning process, it is also important not to lose sight of the significance of keeping information flowing in the other direction. Internal staff will obviously need to be kept apprised of progress, but it is also important to bear in mind that although most people on campus will be unaware that a strategic planning process is even taking place in the library, others (notably campus administration and, often, other deans) will be. Make sure you are providing updates regularly and tailoring them for internal and for external audiences. These updates do not have to be pushed out to individuals—who may find them annoying—but can be put in a publicly-accessible location where all can see them, and from which any interested party can (within reason) contact key library personnel in order to provide feedback. There should also be a publicly-available timeline document that is updated in real time, as needed.

Here again, it is important to remember that two-way communication with stakeholders need not, and should not, end with the finalization and publication of the strategic planning report. As noted above, implementation of the plan and its changes will inevitably result in unintended consequences—some of them happy, and some of them less so. These, like the feedback gathered during the planning process, will represent valuable opportunities for organizational learning and growth.

Pain Management and Reorganization

Implementation of a new strategic plan will, almost inevitably, result in some degree of reorganization and restructuring. This will almost certainly be the most wrenching and difficult part of the process for library staff and must be handled with great sensitivity—though not indecisively. Library leaders should not apologize for making changes that, after all due diligence, they have determined to be in the best interest of the library and, most importantly, its patrons. At the same time, anticipation of the pain that reorganization will inevitably cause should inform all the preplanning, planning, and implementation of the strategic plan: at no point should library leaders lose sight of what the anticipated changes are going to mean for staff. Listening to staff does not mean—and obviously cannot mean—that everyone gets everything they want or that the outcome will be equally acceptable to everyone. But it does mean that input from staff will be considered carefully, and it should mean that when the changes have been announced, their strategic necessity will have been clearly and repeatedly explained.

But what about the pain? Here it is important to stress that although library leaders need to be clear and decisive, they should never be callous or uncaring, and they need to be very careful not to accidentally convey callousness or a lack of care for the impact that strategic reorganization will have on staff. Although the changes themselves may be non-negotiable, resources can and should be made available to help staff deal with them. In some cases, timelines might be flexible and might be stretched in order to ease the impact of the changes.

Assessment

Once full implementation of the strategic plan and its attendant changes has been accomplished, it will be tempting to think that the work is done. But of course, this is not the case: a strategic plan that has not been subjected to critical assessment is a strategic plan that is not complete. And because such assessment must be ongoing to be effective, it is fair to say that strategic planning never ends. There is no need to despair, however. Assessment is simply an integral part of the work libraries do every day, and the effectiveness of a strategic plan is only one of the myriad things that should be assessed on an ongoing basis.

In the specific context of strategic planning, assessment means reflectively asking two levels of question:

- As time goes on, is the current strategic plan continuing to move the library (and its host institution) forward in the ways envisioned and intended?
- Is the library, in its policies, programs, and practices, staying true to the vision and goals of the strategic plan?

If the answer to either of these questions is "no," then the next—very important—question will be: what needs to change—the library, or the strategic plan?

And if the answer is "the latter," then it may well be that the time has come to begin the whole process over again.

Conclusion

There is no question that strategic planning is one of the most difficult, complex, and exhausting projects that any library will take on. If done correctly, it will draw extensively on the library's resources of time, money, energy, and morale; if done incorrectly, it will still draw on those resources, but will also yield a poor outcome. Despite the risks, however, the benefits of undertaking this exercise are considerable: a renewed focus on the library's goals and its alignment with the patrons and the institution it serves; a refreshed set of goals and priorities; more effective and efficient workflows; policies and practices that have been adjusted to reflect new priorities and new external realities. Strategic planning is an essential tool for any academic library that wishes to remain relevant and mission-critical in a constantly-changing landscape.

Appendixes

A Vision for Our Users, a Vision for Ourselves

MARRIOTT LIBRARY STRATEGIC PLAN
2011–2013

Introduction

For much of the 20th century research libraries were known and valued for their collections, and our defining role was to be "a repository of knowledge." Although libraries continue to build and deliver a large collection of resources, we are now defined by the services we offer and our ability to make the work of our users more productive in all areas of teaching, learning and research. The 21st century research library has transformed from delivering services and collections based primarily on what they have in hand and on site to what they can get their hands on, and from what they can do alone to what they can make happen alone and collectively to the benefit of scholars everywhere. Libraries have become a connection point and major player on their campuses.

The 21st century Marriott Library reflects this profound shift in thinking about the role of libraries. It has become an agent of transformation, development, growth and opportunity. It is a center for innovation, an anchor for projects, and an instigator as well as incubator for collaborations that produce integrated, scalable, extensible, lasting, and powerful results. We supply access to high quality knowledge, coupled with high tech, high touch services that strive to remove the mystery from research and learning. We teach students to be "smart for life," with a solid grounding in critical thinking that will serve them for their entire life experience of finding, utilizing, evaluating, and creating knowledge in their chosen careers and personal lives.

The J. Willard Marriott Library is committed to providing excellent services to the students, faculty, and staff of the University of Utah. We are core to the mission of the university and its goals. The mission we have adopted is *to inspire the creation, discovery and use of knowledge for Utah and the world,* which reflects the ambition to be a world-class service center that encourages and enables the success of all university and scholarly endeavors. More than ever we are integral to the process of knowledge generation, and as an intensively interdisciplinary center, we serve as knowledge commons for the university.

The university's priorities inform all of our work. When President Young arrived these priorities were set: undergraduate experience; internationalization; interdisciplinary research and teaching; and technology transfer. The president has added diversity and community, as well as a new emphasis on providing a signature experience for our students. We will strive to stay aligned with university priorities and abreast of the evolving needs of the university and our users. Our three year plan will capitalize both on the renovation of the physical library and the reconceptualization of our services to realize the exciting future that these transformations have made possible. Our plan will also take us through the end of the capital campaign—an endeavor that is essential to achieving our goals. Finally, the plan reflects our aspirations both for our users and ourselves.

Vision for Our Users

Vision: The library exists to advance the research and educational mission of the university, with a primary focus on the many and diverse members of the community of the University of Utah. Our reach extends farther, however, offering resources to the larger community of citizens and scholars to foster research, service, and development of an informed citizenry. Users of the library expect the library to be easy to navigate, helpful at every turn, up-to-date with technology, have information at the ready, and have resources on hand that meet their needs. However, they also have an expectation that if we don't have something we can get it quickly. Those who can't wait may turn elsewhere. They rely less on us for discovery, but search the web without the understanding that not all things are findable through Google and not all things "googleable" will suit their purposes or are worthy of their time and attention. Their experience with library services—in the building and online—should produce a sense of satisfaction and time well spent.

At the same time the processes of creation and expression of our scientific, social, and humanistic inspirations are culminating in a vast corpus of stunning and even life-changing documents, films, recordings, Web sites, and other media, including software. Digital scholarship is advancing in all disciplines, but at uneven pace. Studies of how scholars behave and of disciplinary norms are revealing that their practices vary greatly, but with the peer reviewed article or book still being the gold standard, particularly for untenured researchers.

Since 2008, the National Institutes of Health (NIH) have mandated that researchers deposit their peer-reviewed, NIH-funded research articles in PubMed Central. The *Federal Research Public Access Act* was introduced in Congress to direct other federal agencies to require the deposit of articles in a certified repository. The National Science Foundation (NSF) is asking for stronger data management plans. These public investments are predicated on the idea that the sharing of research data and publishable, replicable results stimulates additional innovation and discoveries. Such an open system of knowledge demands an infrastructure that will endure well into the future.

We enable our faculty to achieve high levels of productivity and impact in their research and teaching by promoting and providing: easy access to technology and services; the information and knowledge resources they want, when they need them and in the form they want; and an open environment for scholarship and the exchange of ideas. Our students must experience a high level of academic engagement to be successful at the U and in their future careers. The Library imparts skills for life long learning, provides advanced technology services, and serves as a home for research, learning, group work, and socializing.

Strategic Directions

Strategic direction 1: Foster smart people and learning communities:
First and foremost we want our users to feel smart when they interact with library services and the many knowledge resources we create and provide. Gone are the days when libraries were mysterious and closed—we aim to supply access to high quality knowledge, coupled with high tech, high touch services that remove the mystery from research and learning. We want our users to be "smart for life," with a solid grounding that will serve them for their entire life experience of finding, utilizing, evaluating, and creating knowledge, and in building communities of learning. This direction links strongly to the direction of elevating our position and impact on campus and the community.

Goals	Actions
Lead users to good information choices and enable users to be self-sufficient.	• Accelerate and expand our VITL initiative into more courses and programs • Examine effectiveness of online information tools
Provide an exceptional environment for student learning and engagement with knowledge	• Create more internships, scholarships, and assistantships • Provide memorable experiences with more student groups • Partner with Undergraduate Studies (UGS) and U Signature Experience • Offer a test-bed for student innovation in collaboration with the Innovation Scholars Program

Strategic direction 2: Accelerate innovation, research and discovery:
Success in research, teaching and learning requires a powerful combination of good content derived from a broad and deep array of knowledge resources, the technology to discover and deliver the content, public policy advocacy, and activism to create greater access to research results, and strategies to capture and preserve the knowledge created and shared through formal and informal publishing channels. The Library can't possibly acquire and manage everything required—we need to work with partners, rely on extensive networks, and take advantage of commercial enterprises for tools and services that extend our capabilities. At the same time many libraries are bursting at the seams with print collections, and cooperative efforts at preserving print in a shared environment are starting to blossom. Given the strength of our collections and facilities, we need to be in the mix.

Goals	Actions
Drive the knowledge generation process on campus	• Build partnerships with faculty and be included in their grants • Earmark funds for the support of university grant applications, new faculty hires, new centers, institutes, and programs as well as open access initiatives
Shift to user driven, demand driven acquisitions with more targeted collection building and print on demand	• Communicate options to campus to allow for more purchase on demand • Work with publishers to increase the number of front list titles available on the EBM • Work with On Demand Books to improve their search interface

Embed services and resources in all user environments by delivering wherever and however desired	• Increase the library presence on mobile devices • Standardize digital content delivery services so that platforms are consistent • Research the effectiveness of "embedded librarian" programs
Provide infrastructure and processes for creating, disseminating and preserving all forms of knowledge	• Ask more and better questions about how our users perform their work • Create a data curation working group and begin a pilot program • Take a leadership role in addressing preservation issues in the state and region
Influence and participate in local and national decisions, strategies and policies regarding access to information and related legal issues	• Participate in creating an open access policy for the U • Continue partnership with regional and national groups that target scholarly communication as an area of focus • Continue linkages among activities related to scholarly communication, cyberinfrastructure and knowledge management • Ensure the Libraries' presence on campus committees that make decisions about the purchase of information resources and tools
Analyze how the campus gets access to knowledge and manages its research-based intellectual assets	• Investigate campus expenditures and funds for acquiring information resources outside of the libraries • Where departments or other campus entities have licensed information resources for their own use, investigate the possibility of expanding them to campus wide licenses • Re-examine what we fund for the entire campus without compensation • Map out all the repositories on campus that contain research information and data

Strategic direction 3: Exploit the digital and networked environment: Digital technologies have spurred new opportunities for community building, collaboration, sharing collections and information, and conducting our business. New avenues have opened up for faculty and students to do their work and to interact with each other. People and organizations which do not have a strong presence on the network are in danger of becoming invisible, out of the flow of work of researchers and students, and perhaps even irrelevant. At the same time technologies have emerged to facilitate rapid delivery of information both in print and digital form—witness the rise of e-books as well as print on demand. Users may choose a number of formats and work in a variety of environments.

Goals	Actions
Provide more resources and services electronically	• Provide e-books, e-journals as primary content for users • Work with publishers and other providers to improve the e-book experience
Develop strategies, priorities and procedures for building our digital collections	• Digitize collections and share in many venues where the users go • Work to ensure library collections are well placed in search results listings • Preserve existing digital content • Enhance outreach & user experience • Bring together U press ebooks with other digital material to benefit both
Move university press books into the e-books network	• Digitize and process texts where needed • Place more books with online vendors to increase discoverability and sales • Influence the contractual arrangements in online publishing environment • Increase collaboration with other presses and libraries

A Vision for Ourselves

Vision: The Marriott Library is a source of inspiration for our users to achieve their diverse goals. This is not a passive role; rather, the library provides vision, leadership, strategies, and resources that enable our users' success. We want to be known for finding solutions to problems and to making things happen. We want to be first class in everything we do and support our staff in achieving success in their responsibilities. Knowledge is the ultimate equalizer and we will be the premier knowledge support service on campus. Our reach should extend to every community, every culture, and every corner of the globe. We will be at the forefront in providing innovative services and experimenting with new model, along with utilizing strong partnerships to accomplish or goals.

Strategic direction 4: Elevate our position and impact on campus and in the community: The library is the primary service hub for a rich suite of information services and knowledge resources. Our roles have changed and our impact on users is much deeper and broader than in the past. We should ensure that people are aware of all we offer and that our services and roles are recognized. We can be a model of others, given our strengths in collaboration and commitment to exemplary service. Moreover, we want to be integral and essential to a larger community of scholars, learners, and interested public who seek out our services, collections and expertise.

Goals	Actions
Deliver high powered solutions by being tightly integrated with campus programs	• Stay closely aligned with university initiatives • Spend more time with deans and faculty identifying their needs and how we can advance their goals • Harmonize approaches and policies with Eccles and Quinney to enhance the user experience with all three libraries • Showcase users research conducted with the library
Be a model and recognized for our work	• Communicate our work and results more widely in professional journals and conferences • Tell our story on campus in many venues and opportunities • Maintain an online library employee CV to document accomplishments, impact and influence
Offer more opportunities that engage the campus as well as the larger community with important issues	• Hold meaningful lectures and workshops • Sustain successful outreach programs

Strategic direction 5: Plan for continual change: We are in a period of constant change that will continue to influence what we do and demand that we transform ourselves regularly. The Marriott Library is the primary and premiere resource for students and faculty in meeting their information needs, and increasingly their requirements for technology support coupled with content delivery. As such it must continue to stretch and expand its expertise and re-imagine its services in support of the users. Development of a strong and flexible organization that can adapt and change is essential. We will emphasize experimental approaches and look for transformational opportunities. Assessment will guide decisions and inform the implementation of pilot projects and experiments.

GOALS	ACTIONS
Stay strategic in our planning and actions and align with university priorities	• Continually scan the environment, share what we learn, keep up with changes • Assess the strategic plan at regular intervals • Devise a plan for meaningful data collection and analysis • Move away from information silos
Experiment and move faster	• Invigorate the innovation and program enrichment process and concept • Review decision processes and look for barriers to action • Seek and nurture strong partners who want to experiment in the same space

Strategic direction 6: Enhance the organization: Accomplishing our goals requires employees who are educated, focused, motivated, and rewarded for actions taken to move the organization forward.

GOALS	ACTIONS
Sustain a flexible organization with employees who are continually learning and stretching	• Re-establish a formalized librarian mentoring program • Create learning opportunities that address critical organizational needs and support effective performance and personal growth • Emphasize learning as a priority and a performance expectation
Attract, retain, and reward high performers	• Offer competitive starting salaries for local and national recruitments • Fix mid-level compaction in alignment with performance • Recognize high performance with meaningful rewards
Improve accountability measures	• Complete revision of the librarian Retention, Promotion, and Tenure guidelines • Continue to refine the performance management system

	• Incorporate information about outcomes related to contributions to councils, committees, and other groups in performance evaluations • Identify and resolve inequities in workload distribution • Define and clarify accountability measures for all levels and types of staff

Enabling Strategies

Enabling strategy 1: Diversify and increase the financial base: Increasingly we have to go out and get it ourselves, not handed to us. Budget constraints, coupled with higher demands and high inflation on materials, place us in a competitive arena and we must be smarter about seeking funding and how it is allocated and used. The Library is expected to seek private funding to support our existing programs and to underpin new ones.

GOALS	ACTIONS
Meet the $30 million goal of the Capital campaign	• Emphasize the Students First fund • Raise money for the University Press prizes • Step up public relations to our donors • Enhance the effectiveness of the Marriott Library Advisory Board
Generate more revenue	• Increase the activities and results of our business ventures
Obtain more grants for experimentation and Projects	• Identify and leverage strategic opportunities and partnerships

Enabling strategy 2: Attend to sustainability and scalability: The Marriott Library launched a green initiative in 2009 and our work has become a model for the campus. Much work has been done to improve our recycling, use of paper, electricity, etc. We want to be sustainable in projects and services we launch as well. A similar, related issue is scalability. We can't be all things to all people, and we can't provide the same level of service to all of our users, such as giving instruction in person to all students in all classes. We have to find ways to extend our reach and influence with limited resources - and we wish to accomplish the same for the University.

GOALS	ACTIONS
Assess the success of the sustainability efforts	• Identify and begin collecting relevant data
Stay connected and active with campus sustainability initiatives	• Maintain involvement and look for opportunities to increase our impact and • improve our results
Be a solution to scalability of campus services and leveraging scarce resources	• Examine where we can provide scalable services for the campus such as digital • scholarship and research computing
Determine how to sustain programs where demand is growing	• Examine how online information can expand impact and improve scalability • Look for partners and additional funding to enable expansion

Enabling strategy 3: Incorporate assessment and evaluation: Since 2007, the Marriott Library has placed a stronger focus on assessment and evaluation of programs and services. Assessment efforts will help us determine success in completing key actions noted throughout the plan and will provide feasibility data for new programs and services. Evaluation points will provide touchstones throughout the three years of the plan to confirm we are staying on track to achieve our goals.

GOALS	ACTIONS
Determine achievement of goals outlined in the strategic plan	• Establish milestones to gauge progress
Use appropriate assessment methods for project evaluation	• Determine inputs needed to measure success and create appropriate measurement tools
Coordinate assessment efforts on campus	• Create a register of library-related campus assessment sources

Executive Council Strategic Planning Retreat Agenda

Executive Council
Strategic Planning Retreat
February 12, 2014
7:30 A.M.–12:00 noon

GOALS OF THE RETREAT

We will use the retreat to construct a framework on which to build the Library's strategic plan. If time permits, we will also have a general discussion of the budget.

Questions we will address:

1. Why have strategic plans?
2. What can we learn from the recent assessment of the current strategic plan?
3. What kinds of facilitation/facilitators are needed?
4. How can we include stakeholders in the planning process?
5. What time span should our plan incorporate?
6. What do we need/expect to have as a "final product"?
7. How do we build assessment into the plan?
8. How do we build the budget into the plan (or the plan into the budget)?
9. What is a reasonable timeline from start to the "final product"?

Schedule

7:30–8:00 A.M.	Breakfast and discussion of the purpose of the retreat
8:00–8:30	Discuss assessment of current plan
8:30–9:45	Planning for planning: Facilitation, stakeholders, time span
9:45–10:00	Break
10:00–11:00	Discuss the plan: Final product, assessment, budget
11:00–11:15	Create a timeline
11:15–12:00	Budget discussion

University of Utah Strategic Goals

THE UNIVERSITY'S FOUR STRATEGIC GOALS

Promote student success to transform lives

Develop and transfer new knowledge

Engage communities to improve health and quality of life

Ensure long-term viability of the university

THE
UNIVERSITY
OF UTAH®

Marriott Library Strategic Directions
2015–2020

ALL  NEED

J. WILLARD MARRIOTT LIBRARY
STRATEGIC DIRECTIONS 2015-2020

◆ **Promote Student Success to Transform Lives**
  ❖ Creatively use resources and space to meet campus needs
  ❖ Provide seamless and responsive assistance for students

◆ **Develop & Transfer New Knowledge**
  ❖ Create a research hub to support scholarly innovation
  ❖ Foster collaborative partnerships with campus and community

◆ **Ensure Long-Term Viability of the U**
  ❖ Increase development and grant writing
  ❖ Create a culture of assessment

◆ **Improve Health & Quality of Life**
  ❖ Promote a healthy learning and work environment
  ❖ Foster diversity and inclusion

◆ **Increase Awareness of Library Services & Resources**
  ❖ Develop and advance a bold and effective marketing plan
  ❖ Continually include students in strategizing and planning

◆ **Enhance Library Employee Potential**
  ❖ Address salary issues
  ❖ Assess needs and provide training and learning opportunities
  ❖ Provide mentoring for students, staff, and faculty

  J. Willard Marriott Library
THE UNIVERSITY OF UTAH

IRB Approval

INSTITUTIONAL REVIEW BOARD
THE UNIVERSITY OF UTAH

75 South 2000 East Salt Lake City, UT 84112 | 801.581.3655 | IRB@utah.edu

IRB:	IRB_00076288
PI:	Parker Dougherty
Title:	Strategic Planning Process for the Marriott Library FY15

Thank you for submitting your request for approval of this project. The IRB has administratively reviewed your application and has determined on 9/18/2014 that your project does NOT meet the definitions of Human Subjects Research according to Federal regulations. Therefore, IRB oversight is not required or necessary for your project.

DETERMINATION JUSTIFICATION:

The activity is not a systematic investigation designed to develop or contribute to generalizable knowledge.

This determination of non-human subjects research only applies to the project as submitted to the IRB. Since this determination is not an approval, it does not expire or need renewal. Remember that all research involving human subjects must be approved or exempted by the IRB before the research is conducted.

If you have questions about this, please contact our office and we will be happy to assist you. Thank you again for submitting your proposal.

Click IRB_00076288 to view the application.

Please take a moment to complete our customer service survey. We appreciate your opinions and feedback.

University of Utah Survey Tester E-mail

Dear University of Utah Survey Tester:

The J. Willard Marriott Library is currently undertaking a strategic planning process which we are calling **Imagine U: Creating YOUR Library of the Future**. We are gathering input from a broad range of the U community. To that end, we are conducting a web-based survey to assess the current and future information, research, and space needs of the U's faculty, staff, and students. The Library will use the survey results to inform future plans. The Library has contracted with two external consulting groups to conduct the survey.

To assure the quality of the survey, we are conducting a pre-test. We appreciate your assistance in this effort. Testing the survey should take approximately **20–25 minutes.** We are looking for your input in a number of areas.

- Do the survey questions make sense as they are currently phrased?
- Is the SurveyMonkey survey structure set up correctly, for instance, do the skip patterns work?
- Are there any other operational issues with the instrument (i.e., response buttons not working properly, etc.)?
- How long does it take you to complete the survey?

After the test, we will be finalizing the survey and distributing it in late October. At that time, you will have the opportunity to complete the finalized survey.

The survey is available at [*insert URL*]. A PDF copy of the survey is attached to this email. Please test this questionnaire and provide feedback via email by **October 10, 2014**. In your feedback, please list issues as they relate to specific survey questions, as well as any general questions or comments about the survey.

If you have any questions as you complete the test survey, please feel free to email or phone.

Thank you very much for participating in the test of the 2014 University of Utah Library Survey.

IRB

Survey

The J. Willard Marriott Library is currently undertaking a strategic planning process which we are calling Imagine U: Creating YOUR Library of the Future. We are gathering input from a broad range of the U community. To that end, we are conducting a webbased survey to assess the current and future information, research, and space needs of the U's faculty, staff, and students. The Library will use the survey results to inform future plans.

This study has been reviewed by the U's Institutional Review Board (IRB_00076288) and has been classified as nonhuman subjects research. We will not ask you for any personal identifying information during the survey. To further protect the confidentiality of your responses an independent market research firm will tabulate all responses, and findings will only be reported in the aggregate.

Contact the Institutional Review Board (IRB) if you have questions regarding your rights as a research participant. You may also contact the IRB if you have questions, complaints, or concerns that you do not feel you can discuss with Library Administration.

You will be able to go forward and back on this survey, however once you finish this survey you will not be able to re enter. Participation in this survey is voluntary. By taking the survey you are giving your consent to have your feedback, comments, and opinions used in our strategic planning process.

If you wish to be included in the drawing for a choice of one of the following prizes (Xbox One, PlayStation 4, Apple iPad Air 16GB, or GoPro HERO3+: Black Edition) please follow the link at the end of the survey to enter your name and email address. This optional entry form is separate from the survey and submitting this information poses no foreseeable risk to participants.

By taking the survey you are giving your consent to have your feedback, comments, and opinions used in our strategic planning process.

Thank you for participating in this study.

University of Utah Marriott Library Faculty/Staff/Student Library Planning

*1. We are surveying a range of members of the University of Utah community. Please indicate if you are: (select only one response).

○ University of Utah Faculty

○ University of Utah Staff

○ University of Utah Student

○ University of Utah Administration (nonfaculty)

*2. What year are you in your studies?

○ First year undergraduate

○ Second year undergraduate

○ Third year undergraduate

○ Fourth year undergraduate

○ Fifth year undergraduate

○ Graduate Student

○ Other, please describe below

Please describe

3. Please indicate whether you reside in University housing or you are a commuter student.

○ Commuter student

○ Reside on campus single student housing

○ Reside in campus married student housing

*4. Please indicate which college you are affiliated with.

○ Architecture & Planning

○ Business

University of Utah Marriott Library Faculty/Staff/Student Library Planning

○ Dentistry

○ Education

○ Engineering

○ Fine Arts

○ Health

○ Honors College

○ Humanities

○ Law

○ Medicine

○ Mines and Earth Sciences

○ Nursing

○ Pharmacy

○ Science

○ Social and Behavioral Science

○ Social Work

About the Library

Please share with us your experiences using the Marriott Library and its services.

*5. What library services have you used during your visits to the Library? (Select all that apply.)

☐ Borrowing (checking out) books and other materials

☐ Interlibrary loan (borrowing books or other materials from other libraries)

☐ Access online information resources (books, databases, journal articles, etc.)

☐ Access digital collections (including the Mountain West Digital Library, Utah Digital Newspapers)

☐ Access technology equipment (e.g. computers, scanners, printers, etc.)

University of Utah Marriott Library Faculty/Staff/Student Library Planning

☐ Use the Special Collections (including archives, rare books/manuscripts)

☐ Reference librarian assistance, both in person or online

☐ Use the Digital Scholarship Lab (e.g. audio/video studio, etc.)

☐ Use Research Consulting Services

☐ Attend Library programming/events/workshops

☐ Other, please describe below

Please describe

```

```

*6. What activities do you do while in the Library? (Select all that apply.)

☐ Attend a University of Utah course

☐ Teach a University of Utah course

☐ Study alone

☐ Study with a group

☐ Use the Library's computers, printing services and/or copy services

☐ Hang out

☐ Meet with my class

☐ Meet with my instructor

☐ Attend a program/event/workshop

☐ Use the Digital Scholarship Lab (e.g. audio/video studio, etc.)

☐ Other, please describe below

Please describe

```

```

University of Utah Marriott Library Faculty/Staff/Student Library Planning

*7. The Library space supports a variety of purposes including space for books and other collections, individual and quiet study space, group study areas, computing services (including public use computers and video and audio media services), and classrooms for instruction. As the Library plans for the future consideration needs to be given to how space is used in the future. Please indicate if these uses of space should be increased, decreased or remain the same.

	Increase the space for this activity	Decrease the space for this activity	Keep the space the same for this activity
Space for books and other collections	☐	☐	☐
Individual and quiet study space	☐	☐	☐
Group study areas	☐	☐	☐
Computing services	☐	☐	☐
Classrooms for instruction	☐	☐	☐

Please share other ideas you have regarding Library space

Marriott Library's website

Please share with us how you used the different services available at the J. W. Marriott Library's website (http://www.lib.utah.edu/).

University of Utah Marriott Library Faculty/Staff/Student Library Planning

8. How useful do you find the Library's website for each of the following purposes?

	Very useful	Useful	Neutral	Not very useful	Not useful at all	Don't use
Access electronic books	☐	☐	☐	☐	☐	☐
Access electronic journals and databases	☐	☐	☐	☐	☐	☐
Search the Library's catalog	☐	☐	☐	☐	☐	☐
Search the Library's digital collection (e.g. Mountain West Digital Library)	☐	☐	☐	☐	☐	☐
Get information on the Library's hours and services	☐	☐	☐	☐	☐	☐
Access reserve course materials	☐	☐	☐	☐	☐	☐
Ask a librarian for help	☐	☐	☐	☐	☐	☐
Request a book or article through interlibrary loan	☐	☐	☐	☐	☐	☐
I haven't visited the Library's website	☐	☐	☐	☐	☐	☐
Other comments	☐	☐	☐	☐	☐	☐

Other comments about the website

University of Utah Marriott Library Faculty/Staff/Student Library Planning

9. How do you access the Library's website or other online services? (Select all that apply.)

☐ Your own computer/laptop on campus

☐ Your own computer/laptop off campus

☐ Your own mobile device, smartphone, tablet (iPad), laptop,etc.

☐ Campus owned computer/laptop or mobile device

☐ Other, please describe below

Please describe

```



```

J. W. Marriott Library Collections and Services

Please share with us how you use the J. W. Marriott Library's Collections and Services. We are including both print and electronic collections, that you may use both in the Library and from your home or office.

*10. How important are the following collections and/or services to your classwork, teaching and/or research?

	Extremely important	Very important	Neither important nor unimportant	Very unimportant	Not at all important	Don't use
Books in print format	☐	☐	☐	☐	☐	☐
Books in electronic format	☐	☐	☐	☐	☐	☐
Journals in electronic format	☐	☐	☐	☐	☐	☐
Journals in print format	☐	☐	☐	☐	☐	☐

University of Utah Marriott Library Faculty/Staff/Student Library Planning

Electronic databases	☐	☐	☐	☐	☐	☐
Library's digital collections (e.g. Mountain West Digital Library)	☐	☐	☐	☐	☐	☐
Library catalog	☐	☐	☐	☐	☐	☐
Reference assistance online	☐	☐	☐	☐	☐	☐
Assistance at the reference Desk	☐	☐	☐	☐	☐	☐
Special collections/ archives	☐	☐	☐	☐	☐	☐
Digital Scholarship Lab (e.g. audio/ video studios, etc.)	☐	☐	☐	☐	☐	☐
Writing Center	☐	☐	☐	☐	☐	☐
Academic Advising	☐	☐	☐	☐	☐	☐
Other, please describe below	☐	☐	☐	☐	☐	☐

Please describe

University of Utah Marriott Library Faculty/Staff/Student Library Planning

*11. What is your level of satisfaction with the following collections and services?

	Very satisfied	Satisfied	Neutral	Dissatisfied	Very dissatisfied	Don't use this collection
Books in print format	☐	☐	☐	☐	☐	☐
Books in electronic format	☐	☐	☐	☐	☐	☐
Journals in electronic format	☐	☐	☐	☐	☐	☐
Journals in print format	☐	☐	☐	☐	☐	☐
Electronic databases	☐	☐	☐	☐	☐	☐
Library's digital collections (e.g. Mountain West Digital Library)	☐	☐	☐	☐	☐	☐
Library catalog	☐	☐	☐	☐	☐	☐
Special collections/ archives	☐	☐	☐	☐	☐	☐
Other, please describe below	☐	☐	☐	☐	☐	☐

Please describe

12. If the Library had a 10% increase in its library collections (including books, journals, databases, and other information resources in all formats), how would you recommend that it be allocated?

University of Utah Marriott Library Faculty/Staff/Student Library Planning

*13. Academic libraries have traditionally held both a circulating collection and noncirculating collections of rare and unique materials. The Marriott Library has placed many of its lowuse books in a storage faculty attached to the Library building from which they can be checked out on request. When dealing with these kinds of lowuse materials in the future, would it be best for the Library to:

☐ Permanently remove them from the collection and if they are needed in the future, borrow them through interlibrary loan, and use the space for other purposes.

☐ Continue to move the materials into permanent storage and use the space for other purposes.

☐ Have fewer books, but still offer a mix of new/recent and noncirculating books.

☐ Other, please describe below

Please describe

Impact on your learning, scholarship, and/or research

The following questions focus on how the Library's collections and services impact your work and studies.

*14. Please indicate if you are a student, faculty or staff member.

☐ Student

☐ Faculty

☐ Staff

University of Utah Marriott Library Faculty/Staff/Student Library Planning

*15. How important are Library collections and services in your studies/work?

	Extremely important	Very important	Neither important nor unimportant	Very unimportant	Not at all Important	Don't know
Access to technology (Knowledge Commons, 3D Printing, Espresso Book-Machine, etc.)	☐	☐	☐	☐	☐	☐
Achieving academic success	☐	☐	☐	☐	☐	☐
Digital Scholarship Lab (e.g. Audio/video Studio, etc.)	☐	☐	☐	☐	☐	☐
Expanding my general knowledge	☐	☐	☐	☐	☐	☐
Finding information to support research assignments and papers	☐	☐	☐	☐	☐	☐
Group study space	☐	☐	☐	☐	☐	☐
Improving my social life	☐	☐	☐	☐	☐	☐
Journal publishing service	☐	☐	☐	☐	☐	☐
Making efficient use of my time	☐	☐	☐	☐	☐	☐
Printing/copying service	☐	☐	☐	☐	☐	☐
Quiet study space	☐	☐	☐	☐	☐	☐

University of Utah Marriott Library Faculty/Staff/Student Library Planning

Wireless access	☐	☐	☐	☐	☐	☐
Other please describe below	☐	☐	☐	☐	☐	☐

Please describe

[ ]

*16. How important are Library collections and services in your research/work?

	Extremely important	Very important	Neither important nor unimportant	Very unimportant	Not at all Important	Don't know
Access to technology (Knowledge Commons, 3D printing, Espresso Book Machine, etc.)	☐	☐	☐	☐	☐	☐
Books/electronic resources in support of my research	☐	☐	☐	☐	☐	☐
Books/electronic resources in support of teaching/student assignments	☐	☐	☐	☐	☐	☐
Using the Library space to meet with students	☐	☐	☐	☐	☐	☐
Digital Scholarship Lab (e.g. Audio/Video studio, etc.)	☐	☐	☐	☐	☐	☐
Depositing research/ publications in the University's institutional repository	☐	☐	☐	☐	☐	☐
Group study	☐	☐	☐	☐	☐	☐

(Cont.)

University of Utah Marriott Library Faculty/Staff/Student Library Planning

	Extremely important	Very important	Neither important nor unimportant	Very unimportant	Not at all Important	Don't know
Quiet study	☐	☐	☐	☐	☐	☐
Printing/copying service	☐	☐	☐	☐	☐	☐
Wireless Access	☐	☐	☐	☐	☐	☐
Ask your librarian to provide instruction in use of library resources/ information literacy	☐	☐	☐	☐	☐	☐
Other, please describe below	☐	☐	☐	☐	☐	☐

Please describe

17. The Library has a positive impact on University of Utah student success.

☐ Strongly agree

☐ Agree

☐ Neither agree nor disagree

☐ Disagree

☐ Strongly disagree

Please describe

University of Utah Marriott Library Faculty/Staff/Student Library Planning

*18. How do you learn about library services and activities?

☐ Campus newsletter

☐ Library newsletter

☐ Library liaison

☐ Word of mouth

☐ Announcements on the Library's website

☐ Email notices

☐ I don't know

Please describe

```



```

Future services

*19. What future services would you use if the Library offered them? (Select all that apply.)

☐ Math lab

☐ GIS lab

☐ Support for statistical analysis including training

☐ Funding in support of Open Access

☐ Expand technology checkout program

☐ Assistance with research data management

☐ Permanent hacker space/maker space program

Please describe

```



```

University of Utah Marriott Library Faculty/Staff/Student Library Planning

20. What are your unmet technology needs?

21. If the Library created a Maker Space Center, how would use the Space to enhance your teaching, learning and/or scholarship?

22. If the Library had a 10% increase in its budget what should the money be spent on?

23. If there was one thing that you would change about the Marriott Library what would it be?

24. What is your overall satisfaction with the Marriott Library?

☐ Very satisfied

☐ Satisfied

☐ Neutral

☐ Dissatisfied

☐ Very dissatisfied

Comment

University of Utah Marriott Library Faculty/Staff/Student Library Planning

Thank you for participating in the survey

The J. W. Marriott Library thanks you for participating in this survey. If you wish to be included in the drawing for a choice of one of the following prizes (Xbox One, PlayStation 4, Apple iPad Air 16GB, or GoPro HERO3+: Black Edition) please follow the link XXXX to enter your name and email address. This optional entry form is separate from the survey and submitting this information poses no foreseeable risk to participants.

Consent Cover Letter for Survey

Imagine U: Creating YOUR Library of the Future

The J. Willard Marriott Library is currently undertaking a strategic planning process, which we are calling **Imagine U: Creating YOUR Library of the Future.** We are gathering input from a broad range of the U community. To that end, we are conducting a web-based survey to assess the current and future information, research, and space needs of the U's faculty, staff, and students. The Library will use the survey results to inform future plans.

Please take the opportunity to complete this short survey before **November 11, 2014.** The survey is available at [*insert URL*].

This study has been reviewed by the U's Institutional Review Board and has been classified as non-human subjects research. We will not ask you for any personal identifying information during the survey. To further protect the confidentiality of your responses, an independent market research firm will tabulate all responses, and findings will only be reported in the aggregate.

If you wish to be included in the drawing for a choice of one of the following prizes (Xbox One, PlayStation 4, Apple iPad Air 16GB, or GoPro HER03+: Black Edition), please follow the link at the end of the survey to enter your name and email address. This optional entry form is separate from the survey and submitting this information poses no foreseeable risk to participants. We welcome your feedback and encourage you to respond freely when answering the survey questions.

If you have any questions, concerns, or complaints about the survey please contact Marriott Library Administration.

Contact the Institutional Review Board (IRB) if you have questions regarding your rights as a research participant. You may also contact the IRB if you have questions, complaints, or concerns that you do not feel you can discuss with Library Administration. The University of Utah IRB may be reached by phone or by e-mail.

Participation in this survey is voluntary. By taking the survey you are giving your consent to have your feedback, comments, and opinions used in our strategic planning process.

Thank you for participating in this study.

Final Report and Recommendations

"Imagine U: Creating YOUR
Library of the Future" Library
Strategic Planning Project

Final Report and Recommendations

Prepared by Tom Clareson, LYRASIS
and Liz Bishoff, The Bishoff Group   3/10/15

Executive Summary

The University of Utah J. Willard Marriott Library initiated a strategic planning process called **Imagine U: Creating YOUR Library of the Future** in Fall 2014. To prepare for the process, the Library developed a planning project to gather input from a broad range of the University community. Project consultants conducted two web-based surveys: one to assess the current and future information, research, and space needs of the University's faculty, staff, administration, and students; the other to gain feedback from Library employees on library programs and perceptions of Library user needs.

In addition, the consultants conducted a series of focus groups with members of the University and Library community to document the needs of both communities, use of current library services, and identification of future library services. The Library will use the focus group and survey results to inform future plans.

The participation levels for both the survey and the focus groups were exceptional, with responses from across the entire University community. The survey was in the field for three weeks with more than 3200 responses (467 of which were from the Medical Campus), and more than 90 individuals participated in the focus group sessions.

The consultants analyzed the findings and developed recommendations dealing with issues including current services, collections, space issues, technology, new services, and awareness and advocacy issues.

Among the key recommendations:

- As the Library continues to evaluate space allocation, the need for expanded individual/quiet study and group study space requires attention.
- In exploring opportunities for new services, expansion of the Technology Checkout Program, implementation of Research Data Management, and support for Open Publishing should all be given consideration.
- Projects to build awareness of the wide spectrum of services, utilizing the many Library advocates among the University of Utah community, can result in more usage of services and resources and further positive response to the Library's offerings.
- Survey responses suggest that patrons would like to see more spending on printed books and e-books, as well as e-journals and electronic databases.

- Opportunities need to be explored for creating new reference-type services that better fit the needs of today's students and faculty.

Introduction

In 2014, the University of Utah J. Willard Marriott Library initiated a strategic planning process called **Imagine U: Creating YOUR Library of the Future**. To prepare for the process, the Library developed a planning project to gather input from a broad range of the University community. To that end, the Library contracted with consultants Tom Clareson (LYRASIS) and Liz Bishoff (The Bishoff Group) to collect data to inform the planning. The project consultants conducted two web-based surveys: one to assess the current and future information, research, and space needs of the University's faculty, staff, administration, and students; the other to gain feedback from Library employees on library programs and perceptions of Library user needs. In addition, the consultants conducted a series of focus groups with members of the University and Library community, to document the overall needs of both the University Community and the Library Employee Community, use of current library services, and identification of future library services. The Library will use the focus group and survey results to inform future plans.

The overall goals of the project were to provide the widest possible input into the development of the J. Willard Marriott Library's Strategic Plan; to gather data and input from across the University of Utah community and Library employees regarding current and future Library services; and to identify key findings and recommendations that will aide in the development of the Marriott Library's strategic plan.

The participation levels for both the survey and the focus groups were exceptional, with responses from across the entire University community—all academic departments, and both undergraduate and graduate students. The survey was in the field for three weeks with 3232 responses (467 from the Medical Campus), and more than 90 individuals participated in the focus group sessions.

The report below features Strategic Planning Recommendations based on Survey and Focus Group results; Key Findings from the Library User and Library Employee Surveys held in October-November 2014; and Key Findings from the focus groups on the project held in September 2014.

University of Utah Marriott Library Strategic Planning Recommendations

From the responses to the Library Employee and Student/Faculty/Staff/Administration surveys, as well as from the focus group discussions, a number of recommendations for future work to improve the productivity of and user experience from the J. Willard Marriott Library became clear:

Current Services: The University of Utah user community had very positive opinions on the current services offered by the Library. Accessing online information, borrowing (checking out) books and other materials, and access to technology equipment were highly rated among all user populations. Reference librarian assistance was utilized by a large portion of the faculty and administration survey participants, but not as highly used by student and staff respondents;

Recommendation: Opportunities need to be explored for creating new reference-type services that better fit the needs of today's students and faculty.

Collections: Library users and employees were unified in their support for continuing to move materials to the ARC storage facility. In addition, when asked how to spend additional library budget funding if it became available, books (print and e-books) were identified by all user groups as the first area of importance for acquisition, and electronic journals and databases were also indicated as areas for potential collection increases.

Recommendation: Continue to move low-use materials to the ARC. If there is a budget increase, allocate more resources to the collection budget—print and e-books, e-journals, and databases.

Library Space: In both survey responses and focus group discussions, the need to increase space for group and individual study scored high. This was also the most prevalent response to an open-ended survey question on things users would like to change about the Library if they could. Focus group discussion included comments on the need for further space and policies dealing with Special Collections materials. Issues of addition of affiliated services and use of classroom space in the Library were also mentioned in focus group discussions and survey comments.

Recommendation: As the Library continues to evaluate space allocation, the need for expanded individual/quiet study and group study space requires attention. Review space allocation for Special Collections, and review the Special Collections Collection Development Policy for issues that could ease space constraints. When there is the possibility of adding affiliated services, review library space needs first, and focus on affiliated services which will provide students with more opportunity for academic success. Finally, review the criteria for determining priorities for the use of classrooms located in the Library.

Technology and Technical Capacity: While the User Focus Groups (especially with College Faculty) and Library Employee Survey indicated some concern with the difficulty of using the Library's catalog, the user survey of students, faculty, staff, and administration gave a generally positive evaluation of this service. Access to, and being able to take advantage of support of technology services were two of the top areas of user need.

Recommendations: Continue offering access to technology through the Library Knowledge Commons. Expand promotion of the Digital Scholarship Lab, as a lack of awareness of this service was discovered in both the focus groups and surveys. Develop support for research data management. Continue to support wireless access. Have trained staff available to support technology services. And, when considering implementation of services that may also be available at other locations on campus, make sure that it makes sense for the Library to offer these services; avoid unnecessary duplication.

New and Future Services: There was agreement between all types of survey respondents that assistance with Research Data Management was important, as was the expansion of the Library Technology checkout program. Statistical analysis support, and funding in support of open access publishing were also highly rated by survey participants; these four areas are top candidates to be further developed as new Marriott Library programs.

Recommendations: As the Library explores opportunities for new services, focus on the services that students and faculty identified as most needed. Expansion of the Technology Checkout Program, implementation of Research Data Management and support, statistical analysis assistance, and support for open access publishing should all be given consideration.

Advocacy/Awareness/Marketing: Particularly in the focus group sessions, but in many of the survey comments as well, it was felt that the Library needs to continue marketing and promoting its services to build awareness of the full spectrum of excellent programs it offers. The consultants particularly liked the idea of development of a "Library Ambassador Program" utilizing strong library proponents from the faculty, administration, staff, and the student body.

Recommendations: Projects to build awareness of the wide spectrum of Library services, utilizing the many Library advocates among the University of Utah community, can result in more usage of library services and resources and further positive response to the Library's offerings. When marketing the Library's services, utilize multiple channels and repeated messaging. Finally, go beyond marketing and promoting the Library simply through electronic means, and increase personal outreach through the "Library Ambassador program" and methods that promote the work of Library employees as well as the Library itself.

Library Employee Culture: Utilizing information from the Library Employee Survey, the focus group sessions including Library Employees, and discussions during the consultants' final visit to campus in February, some final key findings and recommendations for further activity with Library Employees were developed.

A total of 73% of Library Employees are Satisfied or Very Satisfied with the Library as a workplace. Library employees show a strong commitment to the Marriott Library's mission. Employees are committed to customer service, especially through the development of innovative, responsive services. And finally, they are strongly committed to continuing the Library's role as the "Heart of the Campus."

Recommendations: Expand transparency in the overall decision-making processes within the Library, and expand the engagement in decision-making to all levels of library employees. Develop a library advocacy program which advocates not only for the role of the Library on campus, but also for the role of Library employees. Continue to address Library employee salary level issues.

Information on the methodologies for the survey and focus group activities and key findings from each of these sessions appear in the report below.

Survey Findings

Methodology and Demographic Results

As part of the J. Willard Marriott Library's strategic planning project, surveys of library status and needs were conducted in mid-October and early November 2014. The survey was developed and analyzed by project consultants Tom Clareson, LYRASIS, and Liz Bishoff, The Bishoff Group.

Two surveys, one for faculty/staff/students/administration, and the other for library employees, were conducted. The surveys expanded on issues identified through the focus group work performed by the consultants at the University of Utah in September 2014. The results of the two surveys and the focus group sessions form the foundation of this final report to the Library Administration and Strategic Planning Task Force.

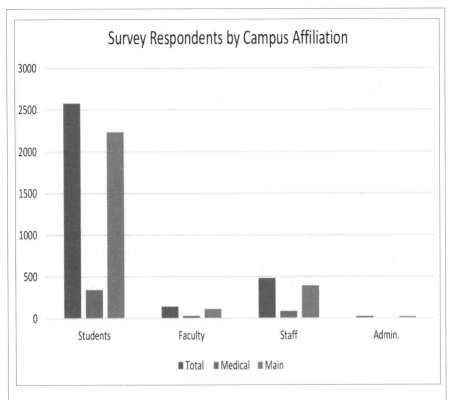

The 3232 total student/faculty/staff/administration survey respondents included 2579 students, 483 staff members, 144 faculty participants, and 24 administrators. The student participants in the survey included 350 first-year undergraduates (14%), 418 second-year undergraduates (19%), 534 third-year undergraduates (21%), 477 fourth-year undergraduates (19%), 283 fifth-year undergraduates (11%), and 268 graduate students (15%). In addition, 14 of the student respondents noted that they had already graduated from the University.

When looking at the results specifically from programs on the Medical Campus, there were 344 students, 88 staff, 31 faculty, and four administrators that responded to the survey. The Medical Campus student participants in the survey included 45 first-year undergraduates (13%), 55 second-year undergraduates (16%), 69 third-year undergraduates (20%), 67 fourth-year undergraduates (19%), 38 fifth-year undergraduates (10%), and 62 graduate students (18%).

The 107 total Library Employee survey respondents included 48 Library staff members (45%), 30 Librarians (28%), 12 student workers (11%), and 8 library managers (7%), as well as 9 respondents who categorized themselves as "other" (8%).

Key Findings from Student/Faculty/Staff/Administration Survey

As part of the University of Utah J. Willard Marriott Library's "Imagine U: Creating YOUR Library of the Future" strategic planning project, a survey on library-related issues was distributed to University students, faculty, staff, and administration between mid-October and early November 2014. A total of 3232 respondents participated in the survey.

Key results from the Student/Faculty/Staff/Administration which the Marriott Library can utilize in their future library planning include:

- A majority of the respondents across all of the survey participant types were satisfied with library services, with a large percentage of students and faculty saying they were very satisfied overall.
- A very positive finding of the survey was that a majority of each of the faculty, staff, and administrator respondent groups, as well as library employees "Strongly Agree" with the statement "The Library has a positive impact on University of Utah student success."

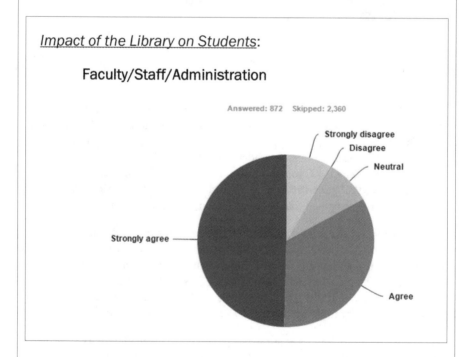

Impact of the Library on Students:

Faculty/Staff/Administration

Answered: 872   Skipped: 2,360

- Strongly disagree
- Disagree
- Neutral
- Agree
- Strongly agree

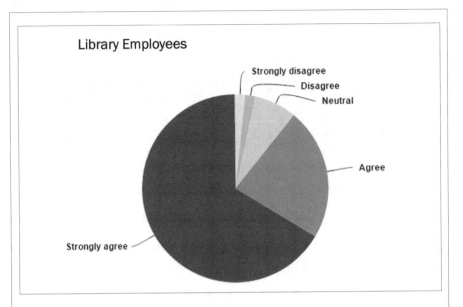

- Top library services utilized by the survey participants included accessing online information, borrowing/checking out materials, access to technological equipment, and reference librarian assistance. Use of group and individual study areas and use of computers, printing, and copy services were top activities by those using the Library.

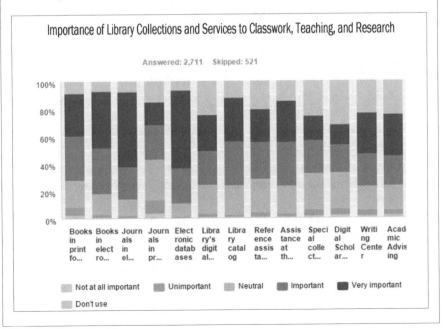

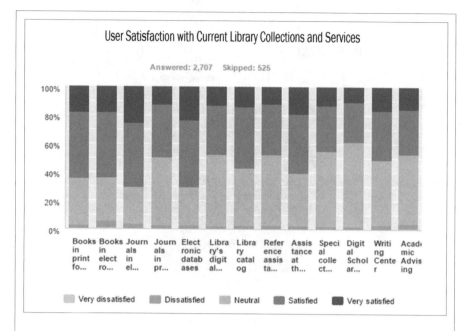

- The "top-ranked" services which were seen as very important across all survey participant types were Journals in Electronic Formats, Electronic Databases, and Books in Electronic Format, and Books in Print Format. These were also the services which survey respondents expressed the most current satisfaction with.

- Wireless access, quiet study space, and finding information to support research assignments and papers were felt by students to be very important to their studies/research/work. Books and electronic resources in support of their research and/or teaching/student assignments were seen as very important by faculty, staff, and administrators.

- Many respondents indicated a desire that the library increase individual and group study spaces.

- Survey respondents overwhelmingly supported moving low use printed materials into permanent storage and using the space for other purposes.

- There was a great deal of agreement across all types of survey respondents that the Library's website was very useful for accessing electronic journals and databases; searching the Library's catalog; getting information on the Library's hours and services; and asking a librarian for help.

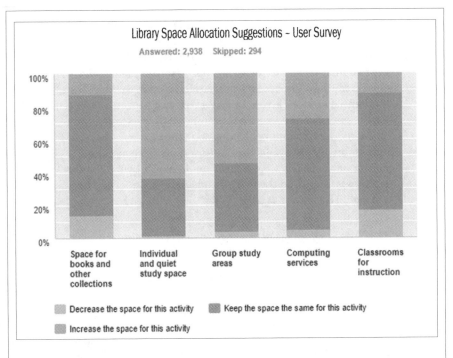

Library Space Allocation Suggestions – User Survey
Answered: 2,938   Skipped: 294

- When asked about unmet technology needs, the majority of the faculty, staff, and student response group members said that their technology needs were being met. Faculty comments reflected need for more electronic journals and books; staff were interested in software instruction and renting or borrowing technology equipment from the library; and students requested better printing services and faster wi-fi. Staff, student, and administrative groups suggested new funding could be used to improve and expand technology offerings.

- In a specific question on a popular new technological development in the Library world, respondents were asked "If the Library created a Maker Space Center, how would you use the space to enhance your teaching, learning, or scholarship?" Across the faculty, staff, and student groups, the largest number of respondents did not know what a maker space was, and wanted more details. Those familiar with this type of service felt that this type of Center would promote group study and learning.

- The most popular methods to gain information about library services across all survey participant groups were Word of Mouth, Email Notices, and Announcements on the Library's website. (The information/promotion channels listed above will be useful in promoting potential future library services.)

- Faculty, staff, and students indicated e- and print books as the first preferred area of increased allocation should the library receive additional funding. Journals were the second most popular format to increase among staff, students, and administration respondents, and databases were the third area of potential increase across faculty, staff, and student survey respondents. An important quote from this survey came from a student: "As a commuter, having so many resources such as journals and books available online for my use when not on campus has been the biggest asset the Marriott Library has had to offer me. I applaud the variety and amount, but expanding on that would be great if at all possible."

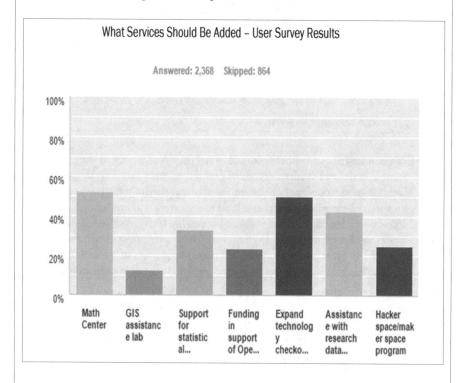

When asked specifically about what services the Library should offer in the future, the largest group was interested in expansion of the technology checkout program; followed closely by assistance with research data management. Support for statistical analysis, and funding in support of open access publishing were also popular, especially among faculty and administrators. The addition of a Math Center was popular with students.

Survey participants were asked "if there was one thing they could change about the Marriott Library, what would it be?" While there were not a large number of faculty comments related to this question, many of those that did comment spoke about expanding access to electronic journals. Staff called for more study space and improved parking for those using the Library. And over 200 students commented on the need for more study space/areas/rooms, particularly focusing on group study.

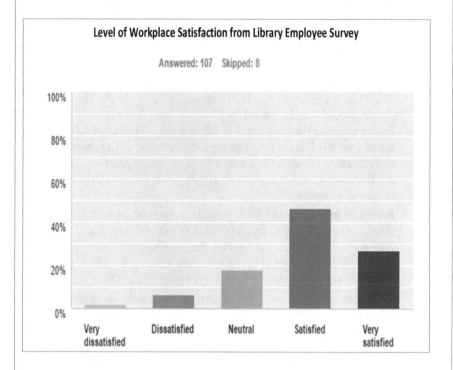

Level of Workplace Satisfaction from Library Employee Survey

Answered: 107   Skipped: 8

Key Findings from Library Employee Survey

- **Overall Workplace Satisfaction:** A total of 73% of the Library employees who responded to the survey were satisfied or very satisfied with Marriott Library as a workplace. There were very few "dissatisfied" or "very dissatisfied" ratings, but nearly 20% of respondents were neutral. Further discussion with employees in individual, committee, and all-staff sessions might be used to move this "neutral" group to being more satisfied.

- **Special Collections**: Library employees believe that users are very satisfied with the Library's Special Collections, and there were a number of survey comments suggesting that this Department should receive more financial and personnel resources to devote to their work. However, there was concern expressed in comments throughout the survey with some Special Collections policies related to limited access to duplicate copies of the same volume, and some of the respondents also feel that Special Collections needs stronger collecting parameters to deal with space limitations now and in the future.

- **Library Catalog**: This service received the most "dissatisfied" and "very dissatisfied" ratings when Library employees were asked about their perception of user satisfaction levels. It also drew the most negative comments, with many Library employees reporting user/patron dissatisfaction with the ability to find items in the catalog. Improving the catalog is also a top suggestion for overall improvement of the Library collections, and is the most-cited activity that "gets in the way of meeting the core needs of Library users." It should be noted that the Library User Survey did not find the same level of dissatisfaction with the Library Catalog among patrons; see the chart and information on the Employee/User survey results similarities

- **Books in print format** are seen by Library employees as important to Library users and were strongly supported in respondent comments throughout the employee survey. Increasing the number of books was the most-cited suggestion from Library employees for improving Library collections.

- **Space Issues** were one of the most talked-about topics in the Focus Groups, and was important to survey participants as well. Library employees believe that additional Group Study Space and Individual Study Space are most greatly desired by patrons. A number of comments in this section showed concern about "outside entities" utilizing Library space. And, while Library employees support continuing to move low-use materials into permanent storage in response to several questions, comments showed concern that these potential "long-tail" resources must remain easily accessible even while in storage. Additionally, providing more study space is seen as a top activity Marriott Library can do to improve support of Library users. Library employee focus group participants also expressed concern about how the classrooms in the Library are allocated, with a recommendation that library instruction should be given higher priority to those classrooms.

- **Technology** is a key area for future services, with the highest number of employee survey respondents interested in offering assistance with research data management and expansion of the technology checkout program.

- **Providing high-quality service** and **advancing the mission of both the Library and University** are seen as top job goals by the largest number of employees.

- There is a strong agreement among Library Employees that **the Library has a positive impact on University of Utah student success**; respondents' agreement with the statement, "The Library is meeting the immediate needs of students and faculty" was a bit more muted. Because there is "an insatiable thirst for resources on campus," more work in evaluating student and faculty needs is necessary.

- **Marketing of Library Services**, both generally and specific to departments such as Special Collections and the Digital Scholarship Lab, is identified as another activity Marriott Library could undertake to improve support of Library users.

- While Library employees noted **difficulty with mediated printing** in response to two separate open-ended questions, they also called for "**reduction or elimination of traditional copy machines**, which are becoming irrelevant with the availability of free scanning and printing services."

- Library employees agree or strongly agree with the statement that they are "**active contributors to the scholarly and creative output of the University of Utah.**"

- In response to the question on how **Library employees can proactively identify improvements that the Library can make**, some comments showed employees having difficulty getting ideas past their supervisors, or showed concern that ideas for improvement are not valued. However, both on this question and in library employees' comments on their overall satisfaction with the Library as a workplace, it was noted that the new Library leadership is increasing trust in acceptance of ideas for improvement, and is helping to "overcome the divide" between Librarians and Library staff.

Comparisons between Library Employee and User Perceptions of Marriott Library

An important outcome of implementing separate surveys of Library Employees and Library Users in this project is that a number of similar questions allowed comparisons between Library Employee perception of a variety of issues at the Library, and the actual feedback from students, faculty, staff, and administrators. The chart below shows a comparison between the top categories mentioned by Library users; other services are discussed and compared in the narrative section below the chart.

Satisfaction with Library Collections and Services:

What Library Employees Think vs. What Library Users Say

Topics	What we think	What users say
Books in print	Very sat/Sat: 69%	Very sat/Sat: 64%
Books in e-format	Very sat/Sat: 50%	Very sat/Sat: 74%
Journals in e-format	Very sat/Sat: 71%	Very sat/Sat: 71%
E-databases	Very sat/Sat: 70%	Very sat/Sat: 71%
Library catalog	Very sat/Sat: 48%	Very sat/Sat: 47%
Lib Digital coll. E.g. MWDL	Very sat/Sat: 52%	Very sat/Sat: 48%
Ref assist online	Very sat/Sat: 57%	Very sat/Sat: 47%
Assist at ref desk	Very sat/Sat: 72%	Very sat/Sat: 61%

Satisfaction with collection and services:

Library Employees: When asked about their perception of user satisfaction with thirteen areas of collection and services offered at the Library, staff felt the highest areas of user satisfaction ("Very Satisfied" ratings) were for Special Collections, Assistance at the Reference Desk, and Electronic Databases. Journals in Print received the highest number of "Neutral" ratings from Library Employees, and, while most respondents rated the Library Catalog as satisfactory, this service did receive the most "Dissatisfied" and "Very Dissatisfied" ratings from Library Employees when judging user perceptions.

Users: When users were asked how satisfied they are with collections and services, there were some distinct differences between their satisfaction and Library Employees' perceptions of it. "Electronic Databases" received a high number of "Very Satisfied" ratings and many "Satisfied" as well. A majority of users also gave "Satisfied" rankings to Books in Print Format, Books in Electronic Format, Journals in Electronic Format, Journals in Print Format, the Library Catalog, Assistance at the Reference Desk, and Electronic Databases. Special Collections/Archives, The Digital Scholarship Lab, the Writing Center, the Library's Digital Collections, and Reference Assistance Online received a number of neutral ratings, and Academic Advising received a majority of Neutral ratings. A goal of the Library should be to review these findings closely and look at how improvements can be made, especially in the areas where direct public services are offered

Comparing the results, the employees' perception of satisfaction for Special Collections was higher than the actual feedback from the users. Also, the users evaluated the Library Catalog to be a better service than Library Employees perceived it to be. While the "Very Satisfied/Satisfied" rate with the Library catalog is very similar, the "Very Dissatisfied/Dissatisfied" rating is quite different. Library employees believe that 28% of users are either very dissatisfied with the catalog and 18% are neutral; in contrast, in the user survey, only 3% (73 users) reported being "Very Dissatisfied" with the Library catalog, and 21% (575) were neutral. Library employees expected only 50% of users would be "Satisfied" or "Very Satisfied" with books in electronic format, but in fact 75% of user reported those levels of satisfaction with ebooks.

Importance of Services to Users:

Library Employees and Users: Another question focused on importance of services to Library users for their classwork, teaching, or research. Here, both in Library Employee perception and across all user survey participants, the top-ranked services that were seen as "Extremely Important" were Journals in

Electronic Format and Electronic Databases. Books in Print format, Assistance at the Reference Desk and the Library Catalog were rated highly by both employees and users (mostly "Important"). Overall, there was good agreement between respondents to both the Employee and User Surveys in this area.

Library Space:

Library Employees and Users: In the question on both surveys about uses of Library space, both the student/faculty/staff/administration survey and the Library employee survey respondents urged increasing space for Group Study Areas, and individual quiet study was also seen as important. Keeping allocations the same for Computing Services and Classrooms for Instruction were also areas of agreement for Library Employees and Users. In a related question on placing low-use books in the ARC storage facility, both employees and users strongly supported continuing to move material into permanent storage and using the space for other purposes.

Users: The users more often suggested keeping the space for books the same; in opposition, a large number of employee survey participants suggested decreasing this activity. Both groups supported moving low-use books and materials to the ARC storage facility.

Future Services:

Library Employees: When asked what services the Library should offer in the future, Library Employees most strongly supported offering assistance with data management and expansion of the technology checkout program.

Users: Users also felt data management and the technology checkout program were the top two areas of future service, but placed the Technology Checkout Program first. Support for statistical analysis and funding in support of open access publishing were also highly-rated potential new services.

Users: A majority of each of the faculty, staff, and administrator respondent groups strongly agreed with this statement, and called the Library "the Heart of the Campus" and a "gathering place" for the campus community.

Library Employees: Finally, in one of the most important questions in the survey, a combined total of nearly 90% of Library Employees saw the Library as having a positive impact on students at the University of Utah.

Focus Group Results

Methodology

As part of the J. Willard Marriott Library's strategic planning project, a series of eight 90 minute in-person focus groups sessions were held on September 23-25, and September 30-October 1, 2014, involving Library Faculty, Library Staff, University Administrators, Academic Faculty and Staff, the Library Executive Council, the Library Strategic Planning Task Force, and undergraduate and graduate students. Approximately 90 individuals from across the University of Utah campus participated in one of the eight focus groups, six of which were conducted by project consultants Liz Bishoff, The Bishoff Group, and Tom Clareson, LYRASIS, and two student focus groups conducted by Marriott Library Learning and Development Manager Melanie Hawks. The objectives of the focus group sessions included:

- Gather input on the University environment, past, current, and future.
- Gather input on the Library environment, past, present, and future.
- Gather library, faculty, student, and staff recommendations for changes to the Library.

The Marriott Library extended invitations to the targeted communities listed above to participate in the 90 minute focus group sessions. Specific focus group discussion guides were prepared for each community and approved by Library Administration and Institutional Review Board. These guides were distributed to the participants in advance of each session to allow them time to consider the questions. Clareson and Bishoff facilitated each session (other than the student focus groups led by Hawks), providing project background, reviewing project objectives, and recording the participant contributions.

Key Focus Group Findings

The key areas of need which the Marriott Library might address in their future library plans include:

- **Library Space:** Groups saw the potential for changes in **Library Space**, including more space for group and individual study. While the size of the general book collections may decrease, an increased focus on Special Collections was called for. Providing and utilizing space for events, such as speaker's commons, was also recommended. The need for fluidity of space and intersections between the various uses of space were also noted.

- **Infrastructure and Technology**: While Administrators mentioned technological infrastructure frustrations that exist across the campus, in the Library there is a concern that the campus is asking for many technological services without funding them, and that while the Library has equipment it is not robust enough to produce what the University community demands. Other **unmet technology needs** included difficulty with audiovisual rights management issues, e-reserves, e-books, and, in some cases, the library catalog. Students asked for better Wi-Fi access and more computer peripherals which could be checked out.

- **Technical capacity**: Many groups expressed concern about storage space on servers, particularly since there is a drive to increase digitization, the increased need to preserve digital content, and the potentially important role of the Library in data management and publishing. (The drive to increase digitization is regarded positively, but there is a feeling it is insufficiently supported on campus.)

- **Key obstacles in doing research/jobs/studies** also included a number of technical issues, such as faculty feeling unable to help students on the wide variety of different technical platforms being used, and the fact that each classroom has a different computer system, making it difficult to know what hardware faculty will need to utilize in the classroom.

- **Collections issues:** Discussion, especially in the Faculty focus group, included the cancellation/loss of journals, transparency of decisions made about library collections, and the inability to browse collections which are in the Library storage facility.

- **Online collection and system concerns,** particularly from faculty, included the ILS system "changing a lot," and the feeling that "many users can't keep up."

- **Where do we need help from the Library**: Areas where the focus group participants expressed a **need for help from the Library** included videos and videoconferencing, copyright issues, graphics, data management, time management, information literacy, grant development, and plotting and statistics assistance and tools. One helpful suggestion was a "Library Reorientation" for faculty and staff, and students could take advantage of this as well.

- **Build Library Advocacy/Awareness**: Across almost all groups there was a recommendation to **expand Library communication/ marketing**. Increasing awareness of 'all the Library has to offer' was seen as important, with recommendations to use multiple marketing channels and repeated messages. Developing a "Library

Ambassador Program" utilizing strong Library proponents from the faculty, administration, staff, and students would be another good marketing activity.

- **The Library and University "Philosophy"** should reflect support for interdisciplinary/multidisciplinary research, a commitment to a culture of assessment and evaluation, and taking stock of everything the Library is doing and if there are things it should stop doing.

- **Leadership**: The Library needs to become a **proactive leader** through greater outreach into the campus community.

- **Workplace issues** are impacting Library morale. Issues raised by staff include low pay for Library staff when compared to campus pay, as well as reallocating responsibilities when not replacing staff, the impact of many upcoming retirements, and micromanagement.

FOCUS GROUP QUESTIONS

Faculty/Staff General Questions

1. What has been the biggest change in your life as a researcher over the past three–five years?
2. Imagine that library space is a pie. How would you divide it between the following six uses: Space for books and other collections, individual/quiet study areas, group study areas, computing services, such as public access computers and instruction?
3. What are your unmet technology needs?

Faculty/Staff Specific Questions

1. In the course of pursuing your research, what obstacles do you currently encounter or expect to encounter in the near future?
2. What problems in teaching do you currently encounter or expect to encounter in the near future?
3. Recognizing that it is important that students understand how to find, evaluate, and ethically use high quality or peer reviewed scholarly works for their course projects, what is the best way to make sure students get that instruction?
4. What library services do you currently use to support your research/teach and use with your students? How can we get information about Library services out to the campus?
5. What do you wish the Marriott Library could offer that would make a difference in your ability to meet the demands of your job?
6. Is there anything else that you would like to share with us about the Marriott Library?

Student General Questions

1. What has been the biggest change in your life transitioning from high school to college (if you are an undergraduate) or from undergraduate to graduate (if you are a graduate)?
2. Imagine that library space is a pie. How would you divide it between the following six uses: space for books and other collections, individual/quiet study areas, group study areas, computers for student use, and instruction?
3. What are your unmet technology needs?

Student Specific Questions

1. What barriers are most frustrating for you when you're doing research?
2. When trying to complete your coursework, what problems do you currently encounter or expect to encounter in the near future?
3. What library services do you currently use to support your studies?
4. What do you wish the Marriott Library could offer that would make a difference in your ability to meet the demands of your studies? How can we get information about Library services out to the campus?
5. Is there anything else that you would like to share with us about the Marriott Library?

Library Employee General Questions

1. What has been the biggest change in your life as a library employee over the past three to five years?
2. Imagine that library space is a pie. How would you divide it between the following six uses: space for books and other collections, individual/quiet study areas, group study areas, computing services, such as public use computers, and instruction, and other?
3. What additional resources, such as technology or training, do you need to be successful in your work?

Library Employee Specific Questions

1. What is the best thing about the Marriott Library?
2. If you could change one thing about the Marriott Library what would it be?
3. What is the one thing that we do best in support of faculty?
4. What is the one thing that we do best in support of students?

5. Based on your interactions with faculty, what do you think is the one thing that they would change about the Marriott Library?
6. Based on your interactions with students, what do you think is the one thing that they would change about the Marriott Library?

Administrator General Questions

1. What has been the biggest change in your life as an academic or administrator over the past three to five years?
2. Imagine that library space is a pie. How would you divide it between the following six uses: space for books and other collections, individual/quiet study areas, group study areas, public use computers, and instruction, and other uses?
3. What are your unmet technology needs?

Administrator Specific Questions

1. Where do your faculty get stuck in the research process?
2. What is the chief complaint from your faculty about teaching?
3. What do you hear from students is the biggest barrier to retention and completion of degrees?
4. Recognizing that it is important that students understand how to find, evaluate, and ethically use high quality or peer reviewed scholarly works for their course projects, what is the best way to make sure students get that instruction?
5. What obstacles do you expect the University to encounter in the near future that will impact the ability to meet its mission and goals?
6. What do you wish the Marriott Library offered that would make a difference in your ability to meet the demands of your job? How can we get information about our Library services out to the campus?
7. What other roles should the Library play in the life of campus?

Prize Acceptance Letter

J. Willard Marriott Library
THE UNIVERSITY OF UTAH

295 South 1500 East Salt Lake City, Utah 84112-0860 (801) 581-8558

I, _____, hereby acknowledge acceptance and possession of the following prize, gift, and/or incentive from the J. Willard Marriott Library:

(Item Description, Item Value)

As an employee of the University of Utah (including University Hospitals & Clinics, University Neuropsychiatric Institute, and University of Utah Research Foundation), I understand that the value of the aforementioned prize, gift, and/or incentive either surpasses certain monetary thresholds as defined in the Internal Revenue Code (IRC) Section 132(e), de minimis fringe benefits, or can be considered cash or cash equivalent and must be reported to the University Tax Services & Payroll Accounting office and recorded as income (additional compensation) for tax purposes. Further information on this policy can be found at: http://fbs.admin.utah.edu/tax-services/common-university-tax-issues/award/

If I am not an employee of the University of Utah, I accept full responsibility to comply with all applicable Internal Revenue Service (IRS) reporting requirements related to my acceptance of the aforementioned prize, gift, and/or incentive.

I understand that I may forgo the required income tax reporting requirement(s) by declining acceptance of the aforementioned prize, gift, and/or incentive.

_____   _____

Signature of Recipient   *Date*

References

Birdsall, Douglas G. 1997. "Strategic Planning in Academic Libraries: A Political Perspective." In *Restructuring Academic Libraries: Organizational Development in the Wake of Technological Change,* edited by Charles A. Schwartz, 253–61. Chicago: Association of College and Research Libraries.

Bolman, Lee G., and Terrence E. Deal. 2013. *Reframing Organizations: Artistry, Choice, and Leadership.* 5th ed. New York: John Wiley and Sons.

Brown, Walter A., and Barbara A. Blake Gonzalez. 2007. "Should Strategic Planning Be Renewed?" *Technical Services Quarterly* 24 (3), 1–14. https://doi.org/ 10.1300/ J124v24n03_01.

Business Dictionary. n.d. "Strategic Planning." http://www.businessdictionary.com/ definition/strategic-planning.html.

Chan, Diana L. H., and Samson C. Soong. 2011. "Strategic Repositioning in a Dynamic Environment." *Library Management* 32 (1/2): 22–36.

Cohen, Alexander, and Elaine Cohen. 2003. "How to Hire the Right Consultant for Your Library." *Computers in Libraries* 23, no. 7 (July/August): 8–12. http://www .infotoday.com/cilmag/ju103/cohen.shtml.

Corrall, Sheila. 2000. *Strategic Management of Information Services: A Planning Handbook.* London: Aslib/IMI.

Dillon, Andrew. 2008. "Accelerating Learning and Discovery: Redefining the Role of Academic Librarians." In *No Brief Candle: Reconceiving Research Libraries for the 21st Century.* Washington, DC: Council on Library and Information Resources.

Franklin, Brinley. 2012. "Surviving to Thriving: Advancing the Institutional Mission." *Journal of Library Administration* 52 (1): 94–107. http://dx.doi.org/10.1080/019 30826.2012.630244.

Germano, Michael A., and Shirley M. Stretch-Stephenson. 2012. "Strategic Value Planning for Libraries." *The Bottom Line: Managing Library Finances* 25 (2): 71–88. https://doi.org/10.1108/08880451211256405.

Heidari-Robinson, Stephen, and Suzanne Heywood. 2016. "Getting Reorgs Right." *Harvard Business Review* 94 (11): 84–89.

Higa-Moore, Mori Lou, Brian Bunnett, Helen G. Mayo, and Cynthia A. Olney. 2002. "Use of Focus Groups in a Library's Strategic Planning Process." *Journal of the Medical Library Association* 90 (1): 86–92.

Hinton, Karen E. 2012. *A Practical Guide to Strategic Planning in Higher Education.* Ann Arbor, MI: Society for College and University Planning.

Jick, Todd D. 2009. "Recipients of Change." In *Organization Change: A Comprehensive Reader,* edited by W. Warner Burke, Dale G. Lake, and Jill Waymire Paine, 404–17. San Francisco: Jossey-Bass.

King Jr., Dwight B. 2005. "User Surveys: Libraries Ask, 'Hey, How Am I Doing?'" *Law Library Journal* 97 (1): 103–15.

Mandeville-Gamble, Steven. 2016. "Communicating and Implementing an Organization Vision." In *Practical Strategies for Academic Library Managers: Leading with Vision through All Levels,* edited by Frances C. Wilkinson and Rebecca L. Lubas, 1–13. Santa Barbara, CA: Libraries Unlimited.

Matthews, Joseph R. 2005. *Strategic Planning and Management for Library Managers.* Westport, CT: Libraries Unlimited.

Meier, John J. 2016. "The Future of Academic Libraries: Conversations with Today's Leaders about Tomorrow." *portal: Libraries and the Academy* 16 (2): 263–88.

McNicol, Sarah. 2005. "The Challenges of Strategic Planning in Academic Libraries." *New Library World* 106 (11/12): 496–509. https://doi.org/10.1108/ 03074800510634982.

McRae, Jerry. 2017. "The Academic Library's Challenges with Stakeholder's Influence in a Digital Age." *AUC Robert W. Woodruff Library Staff Publications* 21, 1–14. http://digitalcommons.auctr.edu/libpubs/21.

Nutefall, Jennifer. 2015. "How an Outside Facilitator Helped Us Create a Better Strategic Plan." *Library Leadership and Management* 29 (3). http:// scholarcommons.scu.edu/library/28.

Nutefall, Jennifer E., and Faye A. Chadwell. 2012. "Preparing for the 21st Century: Academic Library Realignment." *New Library World* 113 (3/4): 162–73. https:// doi.org/10.1108/03074801211218543.

O'Donovan, Dana, and Noah Rimland Flower. 2013. "The Strategic Plan is Dead. Long Live Strategy." *Stanford Social Innovation Review,* January 10, 2013. https://ssir .org/articles/entry/the_strategic_plan_is_dead._long_live_strategy.

Oshry, Barry. 1992. *The Possibilities of Organization.* Boston: Power and Systems.

Saunders, Laura. 2015. "Academic Libraries' Strategic Plans: Top Trends and Under-Recognized Areas." *The Journal of Academic Librarianship* 41, no. 3 (May): 285–91. https://doi.org/10.1016/j.acalib.2015.03.011.

University of Utah. n.d. "Investigator Guidance Series: Exempt Research." Institutional Review Board. https://irb.utah.edu/_pdf/IGS%20-%20Exempt%20Research%20B0314%203.pdf.

About the Authors

RICK ANDERSON is Associate Dean for Collections and Scholarly Communication in the J. Willard Marriott Library at the University of Utah. He has worked previously as a bibliographer for YBP, Inc.; as Head Acquisitions Librarian for the University of North Carolina, Greensboro; and as Director of Resource Acquisition at the University of Nevada, Reno. He serves on numerous editorial and advisory boards and is a regular contributor to *The Scholarly Kitchen*. He has served as president of the North American Serials Interest Group and was the recipient of the HARRASSOWITZ Leadership in Library Acquisitions Award. In 2015 he was elected president of the Society for Scholarly Publishing.

ALBERTA COMER holds an MLS from Indiana University-Bloomington. She has served as Dean and University Librarian at the J. Willard Marriott Library at the University of Utah since 2013 and has served as an officer on the Salt Lake City Public Library's Board of Trustees. Alberta is co-Principal Investigator on a Mellon Foundation grant. She was formerly Library Dean at Cunningham Memorial Library, Indiana State University. Alberta has served as editor of *Indiana Libraries* as well as editor of *Cognotes,* the daily paper of the American Library Association Conference.

HARISH MARINGANTI is Associate Dean for IT and Digital Library Services at the J. Willard Marriott Library. He is responsible for advancing the library's technology initiatives, including strategy, policies, compliance, business processes, and infrastructure. Previously, he served in various roles at Kansas State University Libraries, where he led several technology initiatives. He holds an MS in computing and information sciences and a graduate certificate in organizational leadership from Kansas State University, in addition to a BE from Osmania University, India. Harish is the lead Principal Investigator on an Institute of Museum and Library Services grant. He has also received grants from the Office of Vice President for Research at the University of Utah. While at Kansas State, he was the lead technical architect on a Targeted Excellence grant from the K-State Office of the Provost. His research has appeared in journals including the *Journal of Agricultural and Food Information, Proceedings of TDWG,* and *Proceedings of the 2016 ACM on SIGUCCS Annual Conference.*

CATHERINE SOEHNER is Associate Dean for Research and Learning Services at the University of Utah's J. Willard Marriott Library. She leads a wide range of library services delivered onsite and virtually, including research and information services; library instruction and training for users; and support for faculty, graduate students, and other advanced users in digital scholarship efforts. She has served as Director of the Science and Engineering Libraries at the University of Michigan and Head of the Science and Engineering Library at the University of California Santa Cruz. Her recent presentations and posters have focused on training librarians in data management, marketing library services, methods for effective difficult conversations, and change management. She received her MLS from Indiana University and holds a BS in Nursing from Mount St. Joseph University in Cincinnati, Ohio.

GREGORY C. THOMPSON is Associate Dean of the University of Utah's J. Willard Marriott Library for Special Collections; he is also Adjunct Assistant Professor of History. He received a BS from Colorado State University, BA from Fort Lewis College, and MS and doctoral degrees from the University of Utah. Greg has published several monographs on the Ute tribe, including *Southern Ute Lands, 1848–1899: The Creation of a Reservation* (1972); *The Southern Utes: A Tribal History* (1972); and co-edited with Floyd A. O'Neil, *A History of the Indians of the United States: A Syllabus* (1979). He is a founding member of the Alf Engen Ski Museum Board and serves on the Board of Trustees. His latest publication, with Alan K. Engen, is *First Tracks: A Century of Skiing* (2001), which focuses on the history of skiing in Utah. Greg is also the general editor for the Tanner Trust Publication Series, *Utah, The Mormons, and the West.*

Index